Parks Canada   Parcs Canada

 T5-ARL-658

Welcome to the Rideau Canal

Dear Waterway Visitor:

Welcome to North America's oldest continuously operating waterway. The Rideau Canal National Historic Site is a 202 km corridor of beautiful rivers, lakes and engineered canals linking the towns and cities of Eastern Ontario. Constructed as a military supply route in the early nineteenth century in response to the hostilities of the War of 1812, the canal was immediately recognized as an engineering marvel. It is now a treasured national resource that the world can enjoy. Declared a National Historic Site in 1926 and a Canadian Heritage River in 2000, the Rideau Canal has recently been nominated for inscription as a World Heritage Site.

This guide will prove invaluable to visitors navigating the waters, roads and communities that together make up the Rideau Cultural Heritage Corridor. From Ottawa to Kingston and the communities in between, the corridor is rich with cultural and heritage attractions, arts events, festivals, museums, and galleries. It is becoming increasingly known as an international cultural tourism destination. Explore the corridor and enjoy what the region has to offer.

The Parks Canada Agency is a federal agency that operates and maintains the waterway for the benefit of all Canadians. We pride ourselves on our service to the public. Feel free to ask for information or assistance at any canal lockstation along the waterway. Our staff are experienced and committed to making your journey unforgettable.

Yours truly,

D.C. Stewart
Superintendent
Rideau Canal

Canada

RIDEAU CANAL

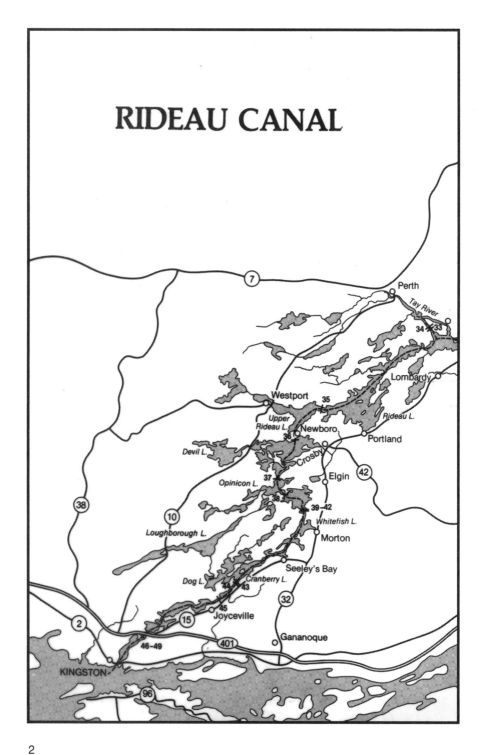

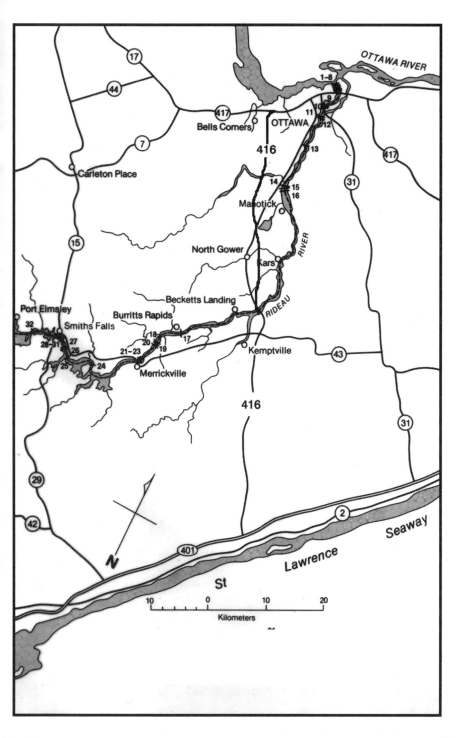

Acknowledgements

We wish to express our thanks to Parks Canada and its staff along the Rideau Canal for their support of this project. Special thanks to **Steve Weir,** Marketing Co-ordinator and **Marc Beaudry**, Tourism Officer, for providing us constant support and advice and maps, pictures and articles. Thanks to **Don MacKay**, the blacksmith at Jones Falls and an experienced kayaker for his article *'Paddling the Rideau Canal.'* Also to **John Coleman**, operations manager at Bellevue House National Historic Site of Canada, for allowing us to print his updated history of the Rideau Canal.

Our appreciation is also extended to Sam Weller of the *Canadian Hydrographic Service* for letting us use their aerial photos of the Rideau. A big thank you to **Ken Watson** for sharing all kinds of great information and for creating the best website ever - www.rideau-info.com. Thanks to **Shari Darling** for her insights on *Summer Grilling Wines*.

We would like to express a special thank you to our advertisers. They have supported the concept of providing a comprehensive directory for visitors to the Rideau Canal and we hope that, in turn, visitors to the Canal will support them.

Published by: Rick & Mary Lyons
Editing, Layout & Design: Jenny Ryan
Account Executive: Glen Dicks
Cover Photos: main photo courtesy of Parks Canada
bottom right: Rowan, Reed, Alexa & Gabby enjoying Canada Day Celebrations on Parliament Hill. Photo Credit- Penny Thompson

Rideau Boating and Road Guide
P.O. Box 1607
Lakefield, ON K0L 2H0
1-800-324-6052 Fax: (705) 652-9694
www.ontariotravelguides.com

Printed and Bound in Canada
ISBN: 0-9681802-6-4

Ontario Travel Guides
1-800-324-6052
www.ontariotravelguides.com

Contents

Articles

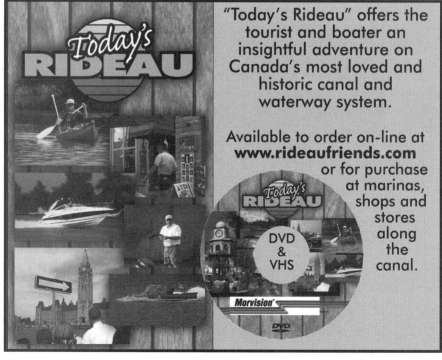

Charts

ℬoaters cruising the Rideau Canal must purchase appropriate charts to help ensure a safe journey. Navigational draught is 5 feet throughout the system and may be shallower at docks. To travel the system Charts 1512 and 1513 are required. These can be obtained by contacting

Friends of the Rideau at 1 Jasper Ave. Smiths Falls, Ontario, K7A 4B5 or call 613-283-5810 www.rideaufriends.com or email:rideaufriends@hotmail.com

For information or a list of chart and publication dealers contact:

Central and Eastern Canada, CHS Chart Distribution Office P.O. Box 8080 830 Industrial Ave, unit 19 Ottawa, ON K1G 3H6 Ph: (613) 998-4931 Fax: (613) 998-1217 Website: www.charts.gc.ca

For CHS publications and a terrific selection of other nautical books contact:

The Chandlery	**The Nautical Mind Bookstore**
367 Poulin Avenue	249 Queen's Quay West
Ottawa, Ontario, K2B 5V2	Toronto, Ontario, M5J 2N5
Ph: (613) 820-7642, 1-800-785-4664	Ph: (416) 203-1163, 1-800-463-9951
Fax: (613) 820-7643	Fax: (416) 203-0729
Email:chandlery@sympatico.ca	Email: books@nauticalmind.com
www.thechandleryonline.com	www.nauticalmind.com

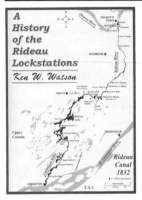

A History of the Rideau Lockstations written by Ken Watson, who since 1996, has run a non-commercial Internet website all about the Rideau. This book has been published by Friends of the Rideau to help bring to the public the interesting details of how these locks were constructed. Friends of the Rideau is a non-profit group dedicated to promoting and enhancing the beautiful Rideau Canal. $18.00

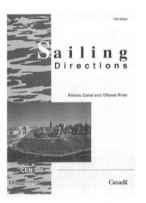

Sailing Directions for the Rideau Canal and Ottawa River. FIRST EDITION (2003) This replaces the very valuable Small Craft Guide to the Rideau, produced by Fisheries and Oceans Canada (Canadian Hydrographic Service). It contains detailed navigation information for the Rideau Canal and Ottawa River, plus interesting historical information. $19.95

A new title published in 2004 *Pathfinders, The Guides of The Rideau* by Ed Bebee. Those intrigued by the social history and cultural fabric of the Rideau will discover an unsung group of men and women who contributed to its flowering. The book is a labour of love by Ed Bebee, an avid fisherman since his youth on Loughborough Lake. Pathfinder's can be ordered through the Friends of the Rideau and proceeds from sales go to Friends of the Rideau. $24.75

Many, if not all Rideau books, old and new, are available through **Friends of the Rideau**, contact them for a list or visit their website for complete details - www.rideaufriends.com or by telephone at (613) 283-5810. Just a few of the many great Rideau 'reads' available:

Rideau Waterway by Robert Legget. The story of how the Rideau was built plus a guide to places of interest along the waterway and much more. 1955. (reprinted in 2001). $19.95

New **The Ferryman's Wife** by Patti Miller. A work of historical fiction about the events surrounding the murder of William Oliver in 1842. Based on the legend of Oliver's Ferry where it is said travelers were murdered in their beds, their bodies hidden beneath the floor-boards. 2004. - $14.95

Building the Rideau Canal: A Pictorial History by Robert Passfield. A 2003 reprint of the 1982 classic. Features 72 period illustrations of the canal during and just following construction. A great Rideau book. 1982. (reprinted in 2003).- $27.95

Rideau Overview

*In the year 2000 the Rideau Canal was designated a **Canadian Heritage River** and became part of the Canadian Heritage River System. This designation is a very important one as it will ensure the Rideau River and its natural and historical beauty will be protected for future generations to discover and enjoy. For more information about the CHRS visit www.chrs.ca. In 2003 the Rideau Canal was shortlisted as a top candidate to become a UNESCO World Heritage Site. 2006 and 2007 will be exceptional years for the Rideau due to the significance of UN heritage recognition and 2007 marks the canal's 175th Anniversary and the creation of a "Rideau Cultural Heritage Corridor" destination.*

Whether a traveller is boating, motoring, hiking or biking, the Rideau corridor proves to be an ideal vacationland. The excellent fishing has been attracting anglers for over a century and the scenic beauty of the lakes and rivers cast a spell on visitors that keeps them coming back again and again. Apart from its natural charm, there are quaint waterway villages and towns to explore, historic sites and museums, fairs, festivals and the metropolitan bustle of Kingston and Ottawa, Canada's capital city.

There is an evident historic appeal to this waterway. The threat of American invasion, though it never did occur, was always present following the War of 1812. The British wanted the security of an inland water route to Kingston to avoid attack by the Americans on the St. Lawrence River. Colonel By and his Royal Engineers were commis-

Repair work at Kingston Mills Dam   Rideau Canal, Parks Canada Archive

sioned to construct a canal system from Ottawa to Kingston to allow British gunboats and supply safe passage from Montreal, through the interior, to Kingston.

The Rideau corridor appears tranquil and pastoral today. It is difficult to imagine the horrors and hardships faced by the early settlers and canal builders. Many of these builders were Irish immigrants forced to quickly adapt to the trials of life in Canada. Other builders were Quebecois who were supplementing their incomes by working on the canal. These hardy souls put in long, hard days of grueling labour. Moreover, the wilds of Upper Canada were rife with black flies and mosquitoes during the summer and many workers and homesteaders were victims of fever and dysentery, later diagnosed as malaria. Those who survived then had to endure the long, lonely isolation of winter. These workers and contributors to the construction of the canal did persevere and accomplished the incredible building of both the canal and settlements.

One will encounter reminders of those early days on a journey through the Rideau system. As an Historic Canal and National Heritage Site, Parks Canada has preserved almost all of the original, manually operated locks. Only three of the forty-seven are operated by electric hydraulics - Smiths Falls Combined, Newboro and Black Rapids.

The four blockhouses, which were strategically built at Kingston Mills, Newboro, the Narrows and Merrickville, have all been restored. Many of the waterway towns and villages, which began as settlements during or before canal construction, have walking tours featuring historic homes and buildings as well as museums or exhibits dedicated to canal history. Visitors will be amazed at how much Canadian history can be absorbed while visiting the Rideau. It is a magical place where past and present live side by side.

Blockhouse Kingston Mills

The trip from Kingston to Ottawa will carry you along the path of the maiden voyage taken by Colonel By and his family. It was May 24th, 1832, the vessel, 'Bytown Pumper' - renamed *Rideau* for the voyage, left Kingston. On May 29th, after many stops at communities on the way, Colonel By sailed into Bytown and thus the Rideau Canal was opened. You will see many of the same sights as Colonel By and his family. Many lockstations have not changed much at all. In many cases, the historic homes, buildings, mills and foundries are still there.

On the Rideau you will follow in the wake of many past Rideau visitors. Commercial vessels used the Rideau for a few years, barges and paddle steamers towing timber and goods, but soon the St. Lawrence became more easily navigated and by 1875 railroads were carrying the bulk of the commercial traffic. The Rideau was used for a time to ship coal for the railway's main junction in Smiths Falls but soon it became cheaper to use trains for that too. Use as a recreational waterway began to be its main purpose. In the early 1900s sport fishing on the Rideau was renown across North America and lodges catering to anglers were built all over the lakes. Soon cottages were springing up and boats with motors began cruising the area, and so marinas were opened. By the 1950s the Rideau looked much as it does today. Recreational boaters in canoes, runabouts, sailboats and cruisers travelling lock to lock enjoying the beauty, tranquility and history of the Rideau.

Ideally the canal will remain a welcome retreat for residents and visitors enjoying its tranquil waters, by boat or from shore. And so we must ensure its existence for future generations by keeping it clean, preserving its habitats and increasing awareness about Canada's living heritage. The canal welcomes visitors because without people to use it, enjoy it and support it, it becomes nothing more than history.

- Be sure to visit the **Bytown Museum** at the Commissariat Building beside the Ottawa Flight Locks. Here you will see many artifacts and documents pertaining to canal construction, the founding of Bytown, now Ottawa, the national capital and Lt. Col. By who was, in his time, never recognized for the magnitude of his efforts to build this canal. It was one of the greatest engineering feats of the 19th century. Celebrate Colonel By Day on the August Holiday Monday at the museum and enjoy heritage activities, free admission to the museum, great fun for the whole family. www.bytownmuseum.com.

Colonel & Lady By, at Colonel By Day Celebrations at the Bytown Museum

Lockmaster's House - Chaffey's Lock

• **The Lockmaster's House** at Chaffey's Lock operated by the Chaffey's Lock Historical Society offers changing exhibits pertaining to the area. It is open from late June to September. The **Blockhouses** at Kingston Mills and Newboro stand open to the public.

• The **Jones Falls Lockstation** offers a great look at Rideau history. Watch the Blacksmith in action at the last remain-

Blacksmith at Jones Falls

Sweeney House, Jones Falls

ing, fully functional blacksmith shop. There is much to see and do here. Take a hike through the woods - you'll find yourself stepping back in time where you can watch and perhaps assist the blacksmith and even purchase a souvenir. A few steps from here you can discover **Sweeney House** and learn more from the costumed guide who will give you a tour of this defensible lockmaster's house. A visit to Jones Falls is a must for any Rideau visitor.

• **The Rideau Canal Museum**, housed in part of the Woods Mill complex in Smiths Falls, offers a unique blend of historic displays and artifacts tracing the building and evolution of the waterway. Also in Smiths Falls is **Heritage House Museum** located beside Old Sly's Locks. It is a restored 1867-75 home recreating the lifestyle of a wealthy mill owner.

• In Merrickville is the **Industrial Heritage Complex**, here an interpretive centre highlights the industrial arts practiced in the village during the 19th Century. It is open to the public during the summer and is operated by Parks Canada.

• Also in Merrickville is the **Blockhouse Museum** adjacent to Lock 21, it features a moat and drawbridge. Though owned by Parks Canada, it has been leased to the Merrickville and District Historical Society. They operate a military and folk museum, open from May to October.

• In Westport visit the **Rideau District Museum.** A former blacksmith forge and carriage shop, it features artifacts of the region's history.

Blockhouse Museum, Merrickville

• The **Perth Museum** at Matheson House, c.1840, offers a glimpse of the lifestyle of well to do families of the Victorian era.

Matheson House
Rideau Canal, Parks Canada Archive

• **Watson's Mill** in Manotick is a 19th Century grist mill still in working condition, operated and managed by the Friends of the Mill. This mill is part of the **Dickinson Square Conservation Area**.

Watson's Mill, Manotick

• In 2004, a historical DVD presentation was introduced by Parks Canada at 4 locations along the Rideau Canal corridor. They can be viewed at **Ottawa, Jones Falls and Kingston Mills** Lockstations and at the **Rideau Canal Museum** in Smiths Falls. The film gives the general history of the Canal and specific history of five lockstations along the corridor.

The Need for a Safe Route to Upper Canada

Article by John Coleman, Operations Manager at Bellevue House National Historic Site of Canada.

The American Revolution created a hostile country to the south of Great Britain's Canadian colonies. For many decades after the establishment of the United States, Americans believed that the conquest of Canada was a piece of unfinished business left over from the revolutionary war. In the event of war the colony of Upper Canada (present-day Ontario) was at particular risk along the St. Lawrence River from Montreal to Kingston. The river route, vital for the transportation of goods and people to and from the Great Lakes area, was easily cut off because much of the southern shore of the river was in American possession.

The need to deal with the weakness of this water link to the Great Lakes became apparent when tensions between Great Britain and the United States led to war in 1812. Canada was fortunate to emerge unscathed after the two year war, but there was a clear recognition that something had to be done to resolve the issue of the vulnerable St. Lawrence River route.

Planning the Rideau Canal System

Following the War of 1812 surveys were carried out to identify a second, safe, route from Montreal to the Great Lakes. The decision was to follow the Ottawa River from Montreal to the mouth of the Rideau River, at present day Ottawa, then travel south along the Rideau and through a series of small lakes to the Cataraqui River which emptied into Lake Ontario at Kingston. Unfortunately, the route selected was navigable only in parts and to use it for boats larger than a canoe necessitated the construction of a series of locks between Ottawa to Kingston. Given the expense of such an undertaking, the project met with little enthusiasm with the British authorities, especially since relations with the United States had returned to normal after the war.

A champion of the building of a canal arose in the person of the Duke of Wellington, famous as the victor over Napoleon at the battle of Waterloo and an influential voice in British politics. The result of his support was the appointment of Lieutenant-Colonel John By of the Royal Engineers to oversee the task of making the Rideau-Cataraqui route into a navigable waterway. By arrived in Canada in 1826 and set up his headquarters near the mouth of the Rideau River. This was the origin of the settlement that was known for many years as Bytown and that eventually was renamed Ottawa. The overall design involved a series of dams and associated locks which would enable boats to travel without impediment from Bytown to Kingston. The original plan for the canal called for the construction of locks that could handle small barges. With considerable foresight, Colonel By boldly advocated a system of much larger locks. He finally persuaded his superiors to authorize the construction of locks with a minimum size of 134 feet long and 33 feet wide, large enough to accommodate the new steamboats which were beginning to appear on the Great Lakes.

The Work and Workers
Work actually began on taming the rivers in 1827. Colonel By and a small contingent of Royal Engineer officers designed the Rideau Canal and supervised the project. The actual construction work was contracted out to private individuals. Most of the locks and dams were built of stone quarried on site, while the necessary iron fixtures were forged by local black-smiths.

The labourers who dug the lock pits, hauled the stones, and built the dams and locks were drawn from two main sources. Many came from the only major populated area in the country, the French-Canadian settlements of Lower Canada. Still others were recruited from the boat-loads of immigrants - mostly from Ireland -

Masonry Crew at Jones Falls
Rideau Canal, Parks Canada Archive

who were beginning to arrive in Canada in ever-increasing numbers. Tragically, new recruits were always needed to replace workers who died from malaria, contracted in the many swamps along the route.

Achievement and Disappointment
The Rideau Canal was officially opened in the summer of 1832. It was an amazing achievement. For most of its length of 202 km, the new canal passed through an unsettled wilderness where By and his workers managed to create forty-seven locks, some of them posing a considerable engineering challenge. Because of its military role, the canal also included defenses in the form of fortified lock masters houses and

substantial blockhouses at the lockstations most exposed to possible enemy attack.

Measured against what was accomplished, the financial cost was low: £ 800,000. But far from applauding the achievement, the British Parliament of 1832 expressed its shock at the expenditure of such a sum of money and recalled By to face a parliamentary inquiry into his activities. While intensive investigation absolved Colonel By of any kind of mismanagement, he never received the honours his achievement should have earned him. He retired to private life, and died a disappointed man in 1836.

The Rise and Fall of the Canal

Although it was constructed as an alternative to the St. Lawrence River in case of war, the new Rideau Canal was more easily navigable than the St. Lawrence River with its series of dangerous rapids between Montreal and Kingston. As a result, after its opening in 1832, it became a busy commercial artery from Montreal to the Great Lakes. But its glory days were short-lived. By 1849, the rapids of the St. Lawrence had been tamed by a series of locks and commercial shippers were quick to switch to this more direct route.

The Rideau Canal's heyday as a busy national highway ended in the 1850s, but the region it passed through remained ill-served by roads and railways until after the First World War, and so the Rideau continued to be an important local transportation system. It was even enlarged during this period, when the Tay Canal was completed in 1887 to connect the town of Perth with the main Rideau system.

After the First World War commercial traffic disappeared almost entirely from the Rideau. It was no longer of any value for military, commercial or transportation purposes. All that saved the system from abandonment was the high cost of taking it apart.

New life for the Rideau

The natural beauty of much of the area through which the canal passes, along with the promise of excellent sport fishing, hunting and recreational boating stimulated the development of the tourism industry in the area and, by the end of the 19th century, hotels and private cottages made their appearance along the canal. Further, in more recent times, the historical value of the canal has become recognized. The canal attracts thousands of visitors every year, anxious to learn about this remarkable engineering achievement and its role in the development of Canada.

Recognizing Canal Builders

Memorials, plaques and Celtic Crosses make for interesting places to visit along the Canal. At Chaffey's Lock a large memorial known as the "Memory Wall" has been erected at one end of the Chaffey's Lock Cemetery (located adjacent to Brown's Marina). Much of the cemetery has been restored in recent years by the Chaffey's Lock and Area Heritage Society. It is an interesting place to visit and a short walk from the Lockstation at Chaffey's.

In Ottawa, located on the east side of the lower locks exists a Celtic Cross. This monument, unveiled on June 27, 2004, was raised by the Rideau Canal Celtic Cross Committee and the Irish Society of Ottawa and the Ottawa and

Memorial Wall at Chaffey's Lock

District Labour Council. A plaque reads: "In Memory of 1000 workers & their families who died building this canal 1826 - 1832." A similar monument was erected in Kingston in 2002, commemorating the canal workers. It is located in Douglas R. Fluhrer Park and overlooks the foot of the Cataraqui River, the southernmost part of the Rideau Canal Waterway. It's inscription reads: "In memory of an estimated one thousand Irish labourers and their co-workers who died of malaria and by accidents in terrible working conditions while building the Rideau Canal, 1826-1832."

Celtic Cross at the Flight Locks in Ottawa, erected June 2004

Merrickville and Newboro are home to cemeteries where many canal workers were buried. Though their graves may be unmarked, plaques have been erected to mark the significance of their lives and contribution to the existence of the Rideau we enjoy today.

Kingston to Newboro

Brewers
Photo Credit: Kevin Fox,
Rideau Canal, Parks Canada

Area 1

Kingston

Where History and Innovation Thrive

Experience *amazing* recreational boating, diving and competitive sailing on Lake Ontario with Kingston's waterfront as the stunning backdrop.

Portsmouth Olympic Harbour

Portsmouth Olympic Harbour was originally constructed for the 21st Olympiad in 1976. Today, the harbour continues to play host to international regattas, its world renowned sailing considered ideal by the boater looking for the adventure of open water.

Flora McDonald Confederation Basin

Located in the heart of downtown Kingston, Flora McDonald Confederation Basin Marina benefits from all that a city centre has to offer. Within easy walking distance you'll find hotels, restaurants, a vibrant night life and a wide variety of shopping opportunities. It is a popular destination for boaters from Toronto, Montreal, Ottawa and many ports in the United States.

To make a reservation contact us today:

City of Kingston Portsmouth Olympic Harbour
53 Yonge Street, Kingston ON K7M 6G4
www.city.kingston.on.ca

Tel: 613-546-4291   E-mail: OlympicHarbour@city.kingston.on.ca

Kingston Harbour, chart 1513-5   *Photo Credit: Canadian Hydrographic Service*

Navigation Notes: The LaSalle Causeway crosses Kingston Harbour, The Cataraqui Bridge (a bascule bridge) spans the cut. It has a clearance of 6 feet/1.8 m when closed and 125 feet/38 m when open. The signal for requesting the bridge to be opened is 3 long blasts followed by 1 short blast.

Kingston

*K*ingston, the largest city of the 1000 Islands region, has the distinction of being the oldest city in Ontario. As early as 1615 explorer Champlain arrived in this area which was then the site of an Iroquois village. By 1673 Comte de Frontenac had established a stronghold here for France which also served as a trading post. Fort Frontenac fell to the British in 1758 and was renamed Kingston after King George III when 1,500 United Empire Loyalists emigrated from the U.S. after the American Revolution. During the War of 1812 Kingston was Upper Canada's major military and naval base and was, therefore, vulnerable to attack. Due to continuing tension between the United States and Britain, the Rideau Canal was built. Fort Henry was completed in 1836 to protect Kingston and the Canal.

Kingston boasts big city excitement and world-class hospitality, shaped by three centuries of proud Canadian heritage. Elegant limestone architecture and historic attractions reveal Kingston's glorious past. There are 17 unique museums to explore. Fort Henry, a National Historic Site, features daily programming May through September, including military drills, exhibits, and the music of the fife and drum.

Kingston City Hall

CITY HALL at 216 Ontario Street has been restored and is open to the public. In 1841, Kingston was considered the logical choice for the capital of Upper and Lower Canada. Prime Minister John A. Macdonald headed Canada's first Parliamentary assembly in Kingston that year. To accommodate this role, architectural plans by George Browne were accepted for a public building in which legislative meetings could be held. As it happened Montreal was instead chosen as capital of the Canadas, thus the new buildings became the Town Hall.

THE MARINE MUSEUM OF THE GREAT LAKES is located at 55 Ontario Street. This has been the site of a shipbuilding yard since 1790. As well as marine history of the Great Lakes, the museum displays models and audio-visual presentations. The *Alexander Henry*, a Canadian Coast Guard Icebreaker, is moored outside the museum and serves as the unique **Aboard Ship Bed & Breakfast** during the warmer months. Call 613-542-2261 for details.

THE PUMPHOUSE STEAM MUSEUM at 23 Ontario Street, is complete with Victorian pumps and other steam operated equipment allowing visitors to relive the era when steam powered the world. There are also 20 custom built model trains, complete with interiors and passengers, on 1200 feet of track with 52 switches.

MURNEY TOWER NATIONAL HISTORIC SITE, located at King and Barrie Streets, was built in 1846 and contains memorabilia and artifacts depicting both military and pioneering life. All the Martello Towers in Kingston were built to defend the town against American invasion. Now, happily, they are restored to attract a tourist invasion.

THE FRONTENAC COUNTY COURT HOUSE at 5 Court Street is another fine example of local limestone construction, built in 1855.

THE MILLER MUSEUM OF GEOLOGY, at 40 Union Street, is open to the public; it may be of interest to those who plan to continue up the Rideau corridor. Visitors may gain a better understanding of the land conditions Colonel By had to contend with during engineering and construction of locks and canals.

BELLEVUE HOUSE NATIONAL HISTORIC SITE at 35 Centre Street, is open to the public from May until September. It was built in 1840 and has been restored to that period. It has the distinction of having been occupied by Sir John A. Macdonald, Canada's first Prime Minister. Visit the exhibit devoted to his career.

Bellevue House

The **PENITENTIARY MUSEUM**, at 55 King Street, is unusually interesting in that it portrays a seamier side of Canadian history. On display are instruments of restraint and torture as well as handmade guns and weapons confiscated from prisoners.

The **INTERNATIONAL HOCKEY HALL OF FAME**, at Alfred and York Streets, reflects Kingston's pride in being the birth place of organized hockey. The first League game was played here in 1885.

The **ROYAL MILITARY COLLEGE OF CANADA MUSEUM & FORT** was originally Fort Frederick, named for General Frederick Haldimand. The college began with a class of 18 cadets in 1876. Its original purpose was to train military leaders to replace troops that were being withdrawn from the newly formed Dominion of Canada.

FORT HENRY NATIONAL HISTORIC SITE, located at the junction of highways #2 and #15, features an exciting military and domestic reenactment of 1860s Canadian history. Daily programming includes costumed guides, fife and drum parades, and displays of 19th Century infantry drills. This majestic citadel has museum rooms filled with artifacts. The spectacular Sunset Ceremonies are held every Wednesday evening in July and August, featuring military precision and musical performances with a fireworks finale. The fort is open daily from mid-May to mid-October, featuring an impressive list of special events each season. Call 613-542-7388 or www.forthenry.com.

Take a "Limestone City" Tour aboard the Confederation Tour Trolley at Confederation Park across from City Hall. For an interesting look at the history of the city try a *Haunted Walk* of Kingston. Call 613-549-6366 for details.

Confederation Tour Trolley

Pick a compass point - the rural landscape surrounding Kingston is a trove of hidden treasures. Roads like the "Old Stagecoach Route", the "Heritage Highway" or "Loyalist Parkway" lead you into a landscape of pastoral rolling hills and mixed forests, speckled with pristine lakes and streams - the backdrop for roadside farmers' markets, artists' studio tours and antique stores. There's great shopping "in-town" too.

Kingston is home to an abundance of interesting **shops** and a wonderful variety of **restaurants,** particularly around the waterfront. This is the old section of town and has managed to retain a quiet, almost colonial atmosphere... during the day. **Dine around the world in a day** - from pubs and patios to international cuisine, Kingston has something to satisfy every palate. Couple your dining experience with a cruise of

the 1000 Islands aboard Ontario's only glass-top ship. After dark, enjoy dancing, live theatre and musical performances. Your home away from home awaits at one of Kingston's diverse accommodation properties - choose from quaint **bed & breakfasts** and charming **inns** to full-service **hotels** and **resorts**, many situated on the beautiful downtown waterfront.

C.O.R.K., Canadian Olympic Regatta Kingston

Kingston has long been a port town and is very popular with the sailing crowd. Because of its constant winds, it has been called a sailor's paradise and to add to its reputation the Portsmouth Harbour was the site of the 1976 Olympic Sailing Events. The Canadian Olympic Regatta Kingston, affectionately called **C.O.R.K.**, is held annually in Portsmouth Harbour each August.

Kingston is also becoming renown for the best fresh-water shipwreck scuba-diving in the world. Hundreds of shipwrecks lie off her shores

Kingston's Flora McDonald Confederation Basin Marina

photo credit: Penny Thompson

Shoal (Martello) Tower at Confederation Basin

Navigation Note: Speed limit is in effect and strictly enforced on Cataraqui River. Stay within channel limits on Colonel By Lake and the River Styx.

and thanks to a tiny creature called the Zebra Mussel, visibility ranges between 30 and 70 feet. Over a dozen of the wrecks are moored to encourage safe diving and conservation.

The **Grand Theatre** at 218 Princess Street, also home to the Kingston Symphony, presents drama, comedy and music all summer long, call 613-530-2050 for box office information. In November and December, there's Kingston's Historic Festival of Lights. The city's thriving community of local performers and artists provide an exciting lineup of cultural activities and special events.

Events to consider when planning your vacation schedule are: **Fanfayre Arts and Crafts Sale**, the **Buskers Rendezvous**, **Limestone City Blues Festival** and the **Dragonboat Festival**.

Call toll-free to help plan your next getaway.
Contact the KINGSTON TOURIST INFORMATION OFFICE at 1-888-855-4555, 613-548-4415 or FAX: 613-548-4549
Email:tourism@kingstoncanada.com or visit their website:
www.kingstoncanada.com

Kingston's official Visitor Information Centre, located in the historic Kingston-Pembroke railway station across from City Hall at 209 Ontario Street.
Main floor tourist information and souvenirs for sale. Washroom facilities accessible from Confederation Park.

Kingston Mills Locks
49-48-47-46

$\mathcal{B}$efore lock construction began, a sawmill and gristmill were located at this site, about four miles inland from Lake Ontario. These mills served the Kingston settlement.

When Colonel By arrived at the gorge to commence construction of this last lock he encountered difficulties. Originally his plans were to build an 11 foot dam upstream of the gorge and excavate a canal to accommodate three locks over the 28 foot drop in elevation. The extreme difficulty of blasting through the hard granite, found along this section of the Cataraqui River, forced By to alter his plans. Instead, he decided to raise the water level by building a 30 foot dam thereby avoiding the lengthy excavation of a river bed. The stone arch dam was constructed and raised the water level sufficiently, thereby flooding the bogs upstream. This also removed some of the threat of malaria from the mosquito breeding grounds. Three combined locks and one detached lock forged the final link in the Rideau system from Ottawa to Kingston.

Although the dam and flood method employed by Colonel By reduced excavation measures, Kingston Mills still required as much blasting as the Newboro lock. These two sets of locks were probably By's most difficult undertakings. The blockhouse was built in 1832 and is one of four built along the Rideau. By had wanted a blockhouse at each lock-site, but this was cost prohibitive. Less costly defensible lockmaster's houses appear elsewhere.

Today, the high granite cliffs surrounding the gorge will have you wondering how Colonel By and his men ever attempted such a gigantic feat. It is worth stopping here to walk along the locks and watch operations. By car you will find this lock approximately 2 kms off Hwy 15. An alternate route is to follow The Old Stage Route, County Road 11 also known as Battersea Road.

Kingston Mills lower locks, Chart 1513-5

photo credit: CHS

The Blockhouse Museum is open during July and August. The original lockmaster's house, The Anglin Centre, features audio-visual presentations outlining the history of Kingston Mills.

If you are arriving by boat, please note that tie up space downstream from the lock is limited. The upstream dock has about 400 feet of tie-up space and camping is also permitted. Charts and passes are available at this lockstation. Approximately three quarters of a mile from the lock, there is a store and snack bar, however, no overnight accommodations are in the vicinity. There is a Farmer's Market located on County Road 21 west of the lockstation.

Kingston Mills Block House

Kingston Mills is an official "Canada Customs Telephone Report Site". It allows U.S. boaters to call directly to Canada Customs to receive a Customs Report Number. It makes visiting the Rideau that much easier. See the boater's handbook section for more details about U.S visitors.

photo credit: Canadian Hydrographic Service   *Kingston Mills, Chart 1513-5*

Colonel By Lake

Isle of Man

Harriet Pt.

River Styx

photo credit: Canadian Hydrographic Service

Isle of Man and Harriet Point, Chart 1513-5

Navigation Note: the channel at Harriet Point connects Colonel By Lake and River Styx, it is a well marked channel but take caution, approaching vessels are often concealed by treelined shores.

Lower Brewers: Lock 45

ower Brewers or Washburn was also a challenging site for workers constructing the lock. The narrow, swampy river created sickening conditions for all who worked here. Samuel Clowes, who had been contracted to build the lock, died of malaria during the attempt. The contract was then given to Robert Drummond, who also completed the lock at Kingston Mills.

The boggy mire of the river bed emitted such a horrible stench that excavation was reported to have been a nauseating experience. These swamplands were the perfect breeding ground for mosquitoes. Thus malaria was introduced into the area. Working on the construction of the Rideau became perilous. It is said that of the 2000 men who laboured on the building of the canal up to 500 lost their lives due to malaria.

The dam which was built at Kingston Mills raised the water level from there to Lower Brewers, thus eliminating the need for locks at Billidore's Rift and Jack's Rift. The lock construction at Washburn was undertaken and completed in great haste to avoid further malaria outbreaks. For this reason many subsequent repairs to the lock were necessary and in 1977 the lock was completely rebuilt. Ample tie-up space is available at each end of the lock.

This is a popular overnight choice for boaters preferring a quiet, undisturbed sleep. The swingbridge has a clearance of 4-5 feet depending on water levels.

This is a secluded and very tranquil lockstation. The closest place for groceries is at Joyceville, 2 miles away. There is also a restaurant in the village. In the fall, the apple orchard, found 100 feet from the

Swing bridge at Lower Brewers

lockstation, opens its sales outlet. Boaters can find gas upstream at marinas located on Cranberry Lake and at Seeley's Bay.

By car this lockstation is found not far off Hwy 15. However a picturesque drive east from County Road 11 on Washburn Road will take you over rolling hills and past tranquil farms to the lockstation and orchard and ultimately Hwy 15.

photo credit: Canadian Hydrographic Service   *Washburn, Chart 1513-4*

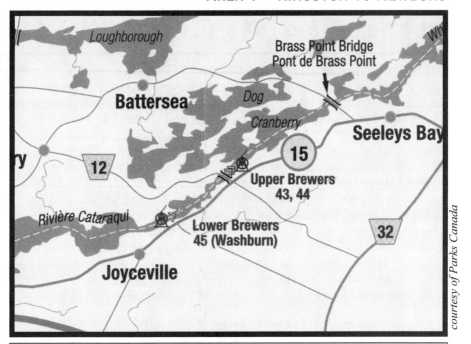

courtesy of Parks Canada

Navigation Note: Don't forget to watch for the profile in rock of the Duke of Wellington, just before you get to Cranberry Lake. It is marked on Chart 1513-4. On approach to Brewers Mills from the North the channel makes a sharp turn at beacon 5206 to avoid the dam.

Brewers Mills, Chart 1513-4   *photo credit: Canadian Hydrographic Service*

M any villages and towns along the Rideau owe their existence and development to canal construction. Some settlements, such as Brewers Mills were once thriving communities that gradually disappeared after construction was completed. Named after John Brewer, who settled here in 1802, this small settlement relied on his sawmill and gristmill. Brewer was contracted to begin lock construction and eventually sold his mills to Colonel By. This acquisition enabled By to build an 18 foot dam where the mill dam had been and Cranberry Marsh was subsequently flooded. The marsh, yet another mosquito haven, was overgrown with cranberry branches which made navigation impossible. In flooding the swamp the vegetation was drowned and thus more easily removed. William Drummond eventually replaced John Brewer as contractor and the two locks and canal works were completed in 1832.

Upper Brewers Lock has ample tie-up space both upstream and down. There is not much of consumer interest in this vicinity. The nearest stop for groceries, hardware, liquor or beer and for dining is at Seeley's Bay about six miles away. Melody Lodge near Brass Point Bridge can provide overnight docking, gas and food. There is also gas available at a nearby campground. Highway 15 is about a half mile from the lock.

Melody Lodge and Marina offers a full service marina as well as barbeque facilities and picnic tables, public phone and data jack for laptop downloading. Fishing licenses and tackle are also available. At Melody you will find cottages, seasonal and transient trailer sites with full service, campsites, seasonal and transient dockage, boat and motor rentals, gas, diesel, pumpout and a mini-store where you will find their famous ice cream!

At marker 222, you can see the Marina, just a mile south-west of the channel on Cranberry Lake, protected from strong winds. They offer you transient docking spaces and so much more in a quiet setting under mature trees.

Full Service Marina

Transient Dockage ~ Groceries & Ice

Diesel & Gas ~ Pump-out

Cottages, Camping & Great Fishing !

Located SW of marker 222.

4328 Melody Lodge Road

R.R.3, Seeley's Bay Ontario K0H 2N0

Phone: (888) MELODY-1 (613) 387-3497

www.melodylodge.ca

Navigation Note: The Round Tail is the NorthWest entrance point to the Cataraqui River from Cranberry Lake.
Cranberry Lake is about 5miles/11kms long. It is noted for good fishing and is scenic cruising grounds, beware of unmarked shoals.

The Dukes Profile

The Round Tail

Cranberry Lake

Photo Credit:Canadian Hydrographic Service

Round Tail btwn Brewers Mills and Cranberry Lake

photo credit: Canadian Hydrographic Service   *Brass Point Bridge, Chart 1513-4*

Navigation Notes: 1)The manually operated swing bridge at Brass Point has a clearance of 4' when closed and opens only during lock operating hours. Refer to Chart 1513-4.
2)Little Cranberry Lake is a 3 mile/6 km long and narrow stretch of water. The channel is well marked but is difficult in places. It requires careful navigation.
3)Stay within channel limits when navigating into Seeley's Bay.

photo credit: Canadian Hydrographic Service   *Seeley's Bay, Chart 1513-4*

Navigation Notes: The hamlet of Morton is situated at Morton's Bay, SE of Pork Islet on Whitefish Lake. The high, wooded cliffs surrounding the bay account for the popularity of this scenic anchorage. A floating dock is located on the east shore of the bay near the dam. Refer to Chart 1513-4.

Seeley's Bay

The flooding of the Cranberry Marsh during the building of the Rideau formed the geographic bay that later became know as Seeley's Bay. The lot on which the village sits was originally granted to Matilda Read. In 1825 it was acquired by her son John Seeley. His father and his family (second wife and younger children) came to live on the land that would become known as the village of Seeley's Bay. Historically the site was a landing for steamboats plying the Rideau. The Seeley family ran a store to serve visitors. It was also a regular stop for stagecoaches travelling between Kingston and Perth.

Located on the east side of Little Cranberry Lake, this small community is a popular stop for supplies. It is the first full service community north of Kingston. Just off Hwy 15, it sits on a bay just a few hundred metres off the main navigation channel. A launch ramp and public dock with hydro are available with overnight and seasonal rates for boats up to 60 feet. This municipal dock is very nice and is just two blocks from the local store. A public park nearby has a playground and washrooms.

There are lots of accommodation choices in the surrounding area. In the village you will find grocery store, beer and liquor store, post office, hardware store, restaurant, bank and medical clinic. A gas station is located 2 km north on Hwy 15. Several marinas are located nearby.

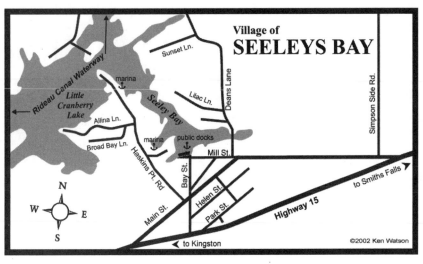

map courtesy of Ken Watson

photo credit: Canadian Hydrographic Service   *Jones Falls-upper, Chart 1513-4*

photo credit: Canadian Hydrographic Service   *Jones Falls from south*

photo credit: Canadian Hydrographic Service   *Jones Falls-lower, Chart 1513-4*

Jones Falls Locks: 42-41-40-39

At the junction of Sand and Whitefish lakes is the quiet, scenic hamlet of Jones Falls. Many tourists visit each summer to enjoy the quiet beauty and to explore the history of the Jones Falls Dam. When built, it was the highest dam of its kind in North America and third highest in the world. This was quite an architectural and engineering feat considering it was built by hand.

Colonel By must have been extremely proud of the work completed here. The huge stone arch dam curves 350 feet from tip to tip. The base is 27-1/2 feet wide and tapers to its summit at 62 feet. The original plans for this site comprised six locks, each lifting ten feet. John Redpath, who later founded a sugar refinery in Montreal, was contracted for the job. When By was informed that the locks would have to be larger than originally planned, he revised the plans. Since there was no room for six locks in the canal, he instead built three combined locks leading to a turning basin and a detached lock past the basin. Each lock then required a lift of 15 feet to compensate for the two omitted locks.

A camp, called Estherville, was established for the 200 men who were employed in this massive undertaking. All the earth was removed by shovel and tons of sandstone had to be brought in from Elgin for the construction. Malaria, the scourge of the Cataraqui, struck a felling blow to every worker here in 1828. For a time, not a single man in camp was well enough to work. In spite of the taxing health conditions, as well as the many deaths, the work was finally completed. The massive dam and four locks have certainly stood the test of time. This impressive site is indicative of the monstrous and remarkable task the building of this canal became.

A visit to the original lockmaster's house will prove most interesting. It is a fine example of a defensible

Information Kiosk at Jones Falls

house. As the cost of the blockhouses was prohibitive, defensible lockmaster houses were built as a less expensive alternative. These were built at strategic points overlooking the locks where the lockmaster could always be ready to fend off marauders and saboteurs. The first lockmaster here, Peter Sweeney, kept a journal during his often lonely vigil at Jones Falls and a copy of it is on display. The house is now an interpretive centre with a costumed guide to answer your questions. The blacksmith's shop nearby has been restored by Parks Canada and is open to the public. During the summer, the village smithy operates his forge as his predecessor did in 1843.

above: blacksmith at work

left: view across the turning basin from blacksmith shop

It is well worth the nature hike around the locks, through woods and across a creek on a wooden bridge to make your way to the Blacksmith Shop and Sweeney House. You can become the blacksmith's apprentice or purchase a handtooled souvenir. It is a great place to spend a day and relive some of the history of the area.

lock 42 at Jones Falls

Bridge at Jones Falls, dock & Hotel Kenney

Another historic point of interest at Jones Falls is the **Hotel Kenney.**
This fine old country inn was built in 1877 and is still operated by the
Kenney family. Here you'll find great accommodations, fishing trips
that can be arranged with an experienced guide, boat rentals and marina facilities. A **convenience store**, newsstand and laundromat are on
site, along with a **coffee shop**, and **dining room** with an excellent
wine cellar. A lovely **gift shop** is located next to the lobby.

It usually takes about one and a half hours to pass through the four
locks and tie-up space is limited. There are many small bays nearby
that can provide suitable anchorage.

A stop at this lockstation is a must for any visitor to the Rideau. By
road or by boat we highly recommend stopping here to experience all
that the Jones Falls Lockstation and Hotel Kenney have to offer.

— Shangri-La Lodge & Marina 613-359-5774
(adjacent to Hotel Kenny) www.shangri.ca

Navigation Note: The narrow winding channel btwn Jones Falls and Eel Bay is
known as The Quarters. Navigate with care as approaching boats will be difficult to
see and at two places there isn't much room to maneuver.

Davis Lock:38

$\mathcal{T}$he land at this locksite belonged to Walter Davis. At the turn of the Nineteenth Century, Davis built a dam and sawmill where canal works now stand. Colonel By was going to bypass the mill but eventually bought the property and constructed a new dam and lock.

It is interesting that this remains a secluded lock where at other sites villages were born. Davis Lock remains as it did 175 years ago. The Lockmaster's house was originally a stone fort erected in reaction to the Upper Canada Rebellion of 1837-38. Built in 1842, this defensible lockmaster's house was recently renovated. It is the best preserved in terms of original architecture of all such houses along the canal.

There are no stores, restaurants or accommodations to be found in the immediate area. Tie-up space is limited and the nearest marina is approximately three miles south.

Davis lock is also known as 'solitude lock'. It is quiet and secluded, located literally at the end of the road, nine kms off Hwy 15. This lock connects Sand Lake to Opinicon Lake.

Opinicon Lake

Davis Lock

Sand Lake

Davis Lock, Chart 1513-3   *photo credit: Canadian Hydrographic Service*

Delta

Delta, though not directly on the Rideau, is just a short drive. It is a charming village located between Upper and Lower Beverly lakes, a quaint settlement with a great deal of spirit. In the early 1800's, Delta was a flourishing farming and industrial community providing a number of smiths, general stores, hotels, a tannery, distillery, brickyard, foundry, cheese factory, carriage works, newspaper and even a hospital. Delta remains a village with a great deal of character, history and beauty. There are a few Bed and Breakfasts within the village which are open year round. Fine dining and luxurious accommodation is offered at the stately Denaut Mansion Country Inn.

One of the most notable attractions in Delta is the Old Stone Mill, built in 1810. It has been designated as a National Historic Site and is the only stone grist mill in Canada that has been given this title. It is a magnificent building. The Mill is open throughout the summer and on weekends throughout the spring and fall for tours of this Museum of Industrial Heritage and Milling Technology. The mill is undergoing a major restoration. It's physical restoration was completed early in 2004 and a grand reopening ceremony took place. Donations to the restoration project are welcomed but admission is free. Also open for visitors is the Old Town Hall museum offering agricultural exhibits and town history.

The annual Delta Fair is one of the oldest agriculturally based rural fairs in Ontario, dating back to 1830. It is held during the last week of July, and is of interest to young and old.

Elgin

A thriving community was established here and the building of the Rideau helped a great deal. Originally known as Halladay's Corners, this village has an interesting history. In the 1830s Mormon missionaries arrived and recruited a number of families in the area. It was from Halladay's Corners that 135 covered wagons left for settlements in the U.S.

Though not directly on the waterway this quiet village makes a nice stop and is within easy driving distance of Davis Lock, Jones Falls and Chaffey's. It becomes a busy place during the summer months, as visitors and cottagers converge to stock up on supplies. The village boasts all the necessary amenities including: grocery store, general store, video store, post office, churches, gas stations, restaurants and a combination liquor and beer store. There is also a bank, pharmacy with bank machine, laundromat, antique store and hardware store.

Though no accommodations are right in the village, Elgin attracts the business of campers and cottagers from all around. Rideau Lakes Township Park at Sand Lake has excellent swimming and picnic facilities. Because Elgin is situated in the heart of dairy farmland, this is the place for cheese lovers. Check out the Forfar Cheese Factory located a few kilometres south. Elgin is also a great place to sample fresh corn from local farmers in August. Special events here include "Elgin Days", held during the second weekend in July each year.

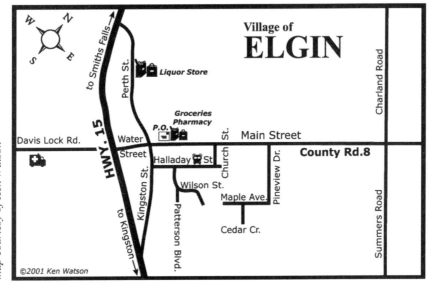

Village of **ELGIN**

map courtesy of Ken Watson

©2001 Ken Watson

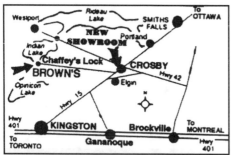

This lock shared the same fate as Upper Brewers. The small settlement, established by Samuel Chaffey, disappeared when canal construction began. Because his gristmill, sawmill, carding mill and distillery were well established and provided good service to neighbouring communities, By intended to circumvent the mill complex. When Chaffey succumbed to malaria, however, his widow sold the mills and surrounding land to By. This simplified construction procedures.

As on the other Cataraqui canal sites, malaria took its toll. Opinicon Lake was formerly called Mosquito Lake, for reasons which were quite obvious in the early 1800s. Many canal workers died and were buried in unmarked graves not far from this lock. This single lock, carrying vessels up almost 11 feet was eventually completed, despite outbreaks of malaria.

Of historical interest is the defensible lockmaster's house built in 1844 as a low-cost substitute for a blockhouse. Originally built as a single storey limestone structure, in 1894 a framed second storey and kitchen were added. From 1844 to 1967 five lockmaster's resided here. A museum was opened in 1984. Here you can enjoy the film "The Golden Years", a 1982 production detailing the hardships and joys of life in early Chaffey's. **The Lockmaster's House Museum**, operated by the Chaffey's Lock and Area Heritage Society, is open from late June to September. Exhibits found here interpret canal life in years gone by.

Painting of the Lockmaster's House Museum by Eleanor Pinsonneault. Visit her studio, Cedars Art Studio, a short walk from the lockstation, where her paintings of many local sites can be viewed and purchased.

There is ample tie-up space at the lock: 200 feet downstream and 120 feet up.

Marina facilities are available close by. At **Brown's Marina** full marine services including repairs, gas, pump-out, dockage with power and the 'Buoys and Toys' store is a short walk from the dock. The Opinicon Resort Marina also provides gas and dockage.

The Opinicon Resort has an interesting history. Originally called Camp Easy in the 1890s, it was later known as the Openacon Club, an exclusive fishing resort. The main part of the building is more than 130 years old. In 1922 the property was purchased by the current owner's family and it has been a haven to tourists and anglers ever since. The Opinicon offers American Plan accommodations in either **hotel** or **cottages**, **fine dining** and recreation as well as **docking** facilities.

Right: A delightful spot to rest and enjoy the view at The Opinicon Resort, the red painted chairs dotting the property will invite you to relax and stay awhile.

It is worth the short walk from the lockstation past Brown's Marina to visit Chaffey's Lock Memory Wall. This wall is a self sustaining project of the Chaffey's Lock and Area Heritage Society, built by community efforts and with the support of Parks Canada.

Gates that mark the entrance to the memory wall and cemetery at Chaffey's Lock

Plaques on the wall, erected by individuals and families, celebrate not only the founders and canal builders but many who have been, or are, part of the continuing life and spirit of Chaffey's Lock and the surrounding area. It is a historic cemetery of unmarked canal builder's graves and a moving memorial. The 'walls' on which the plaques are mounted are in fact Rideau Canal lock gates.

Chaffey's Locks, Chart 1513-3

photo credit: Canadian Hydrographic Service

Navigation Note: Opinicon Lake is a 4 mile/8km stretch with several treed islands, offers great cruising, with few dangerous shoals - many sheltered areas and good temporary anchorages.

Don't miss this little rendezvous with the past. Continue your walk down Chaffey's Lock Road visit Brown's Buoys and Toys Store and then carry on to Cedar's Art Studio. Here you won't be disappointed. Local artist, Eleanor Pinsonneault has some beautiful works for sale and display, many are paintings of area sites and canal locations.

Antique Shop located in the Old Mill at Chaffey's Lock

Across the bridge from the Lockstation and the Lockmaster's House Museum you'll find the Old Mill, now an antique shop definitely worth the short walk across the bridge for an opportunity to find a treasure from yesteryear.

You are likely to see "Chuckles" docked at Chaffey's Lock. Classic Rideau Cruises offers a variety of cruise/boat tour packages that include meals at The Opinicon and overnight accommodations at Portland Bay B&B, see the Cruise section in this guide for details.

Left: Brown's Buoys and Toys store located in Crosby at the intersection of Hwy 15 and 42

47

Newboro

*H*ere at the highest point on the canal, is Newboro. It was earlier called the Isthmus which essentially means passage. Canal construction here was a nightmare. The plague of malaria spreading mosquitoes was so bad that in the summer of 1829 labourers refused to work. William Hartwell originally contracted to complete the work here found blasting through the granite so frustrating that he surrendered his contract. Eventually the site was completed after much human suffering. Newboro's Old Presbyterian Cemetery is home to a monument dedicated to the Sappers and Miners who died here between 1826 and 1832.

During the construction of the canal, many of the Irish immigrants who were brought over for that purpose lived in rather crude shacks nearby. At the north end of Main Street a log hotel was situated. The cleared area around was known as Bully's Acre. It was here the men sometimes engaged in wrestling or boxing and other such forms of settling their disputes. Local lore tells of a Thomas Cassidy who, one St. Patrick's Day, started a fight with a celebrating Irishman which almost turned into a village riot. The fighters dispersed quickly when the guards from the Royal Sappers and Miners charged across "Sappers Bridge" with fixed bayonets. This bridge was located near the stone abutments of the old highway bridge and can be seen when boating through the canal cut.

Loon Village Gift & Antique Shop, Drummond Street, Newboro.

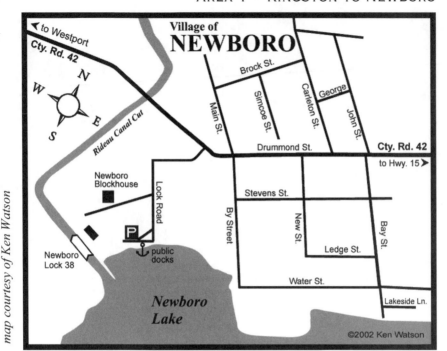

map courtesy of Ken Watson

Newboro can be found on Hwy 42. The village is a popular stop for boaters as it is easily accessible from the lockstation. Supplies are available at the grocery store. Loon Village and other unique spots offer some terrific shopping. A restaurant, post office, medical clinic and bank can also be found in the village. There is a gas dock nearby. Reservations are recommended for accommodation in Newboro. Some of the homes in Newboro date back to the early days so it is well worth taking a walking tour.

If you are boating, the public wharf is a beautiful spot for overnight stays and is only a short walk, past the blockhouse, to all amenities.

From Newboro boaters will travel the narrow granite-bordered channel connecting Newboro Lake to Upper Rideau Lake. At this point boaters are exiting the Cataraqui River System and entering the Rideau River system.

Navigation Note: When getting underway from Newboro, boaters must remember that the buoys will be reversed as Newboro is at the summit of canal waters. Considered the 'home port' - it is upstream from Ottawa to Newboro and it is upstream from Kingston to Newboro.

Newboro, Chart 1513-3   *photo credit: Canadian Hydrographic Service*

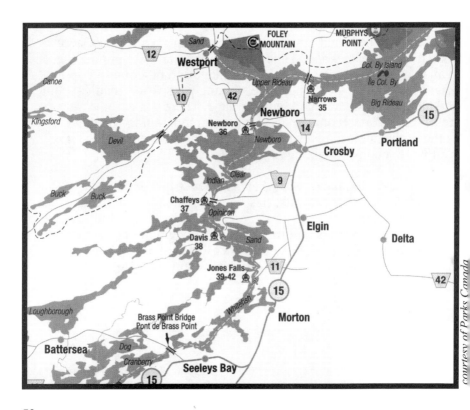

Newboro Lock:36

The site of this lock, between Upper Rideau and Newboro lakes, was one of the most difficult and dangerous canal cuts made. A length of 2.5 km(1.5mi) of canal had to be excavated to join Upper Rideau Lake to Newboro Lake. Unfortunately this land proved to be solid granite.

The rock had to be blown out using gun powder and many men were killed or maimed during this process. Adding insult to injury, malaria again scourged this worksite in 1828, leaving few men able to work. Blasting procedures were slow and laborious and when malaria broke out again the following year, By's entire work force was laid low.

A hospital was erected for the ailing and the 7th Company of Royal Sappers and Miners had to be called in to take over construction. Finally, it was decided to raise the water level of Upper Rideau Lake by building another lock at the narrows, thereby eliminating the need for deeper excavation at Isthmus.

Newboro Lake

Newboro

McNally's Bay

photo credit: Canadian Hydrographic Service   *Newboro from north, Chart 1513-3*

The blockhouse, built in 1832 to house a lock master, could also accommodate 20 guards in the event of a raid. Sabotage at the summit of the waterway would have been the undoing of the entire system. Today this house stands open to summer visitors.

The Old Presbyterian Cemetery lies just to the west of the canal. It was here, in unmarked graves, that the labourers who succumbed to malaria were buried. Between the cemetery site and the canal was the location of the barracks of the 7th Company of the Royal Sappers and Miners.

Newboro is one of the busiest locks on the Rideau. There is tie-up space of approximately 200 feet at each end of the lock, which is a ten minute walk to the village. The public dock in Newboro has docking facilities and a draught of five feet. Gas is available at Stirling Lodge in Newboro. All amenities are available in the village including groceries, hardware, restaurants, shopping and more.

Elbow Channel, Chart 1513-3   *photo credit: Canadian Hydrographic Service*

Navigation Note: Elbow Channel is a natural passage joining Clear Lake and Newboro Lake. The approach from Clear Lake is open and straight. Note a sudden sharp turn at NW end.

Newboro to Smiths Falls

Old Slys
Photo Credit: Simon Lunn,
Rideau Canal, Parks Canada

Area 2

Westport

The village of Westport is located at the foot of Foley Mountain on the west shore of Upper Rideau Lake. It has an interesting history and offers a change of pace to visitors; Westport celebrated its 100th anniversary in 2004. During canal construction, many Irish workers settled in the area and the sawmills of Stoddard and Manhard attracted further settlers.

When stopping at Westport, be sure to visit the **Rideau District Museum** on Bedford Street. The museum was originally the blacksmith's shop and has many interesting artifacts. Available at the museum is a brochure outlining walking tours of the village.

Foley Mountain Conservation Area, which has hiking trails, picnic sites, a beach and an Interpretation Centre, affords a panoramic view of Westport and Upper Rideau Lake from Spy Rock. The **Rideau Trail** passes through the conservation

Westport Spring located at the end of Spring Street off Main. It is a great place to rest a while and enjoy the view of Upper Rideau Lake.

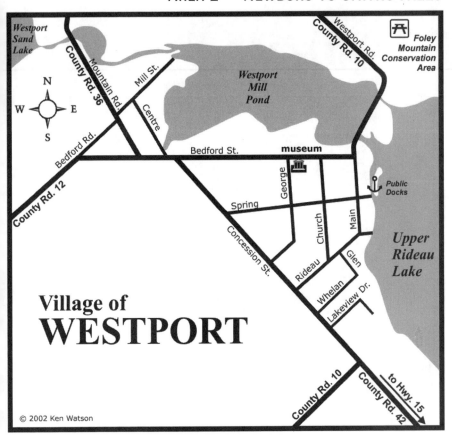

area's 800 acres. Contact Friends of Foley Mountain for information at 613-273-3255. There is also a beach and pavilion on Sand Lake, maintained by the Lions Club, just west of the village.

The **Westport Antique Show**, one of the best in Ontario, takes place the first weekend of June. Canada Day is always a great celebration involving many community groups. Included in the festivities are entertainment, a BBQ and an evening closing fireworks display.

The **Rideau Valley Art Festival,** held every year since 1982, takes place in August. This juried show attracts talented artists and a large attendance. It also generates an array of other art exhibits throughout the village. Go to www.rideaulakes.net/artfest for more details.

Navigation Note: To get to Westport you must leave the main route, you'll find a buoyed channel into Westport along the north shore of Upper Rideau Lake. Upper Rideau Lake is the highest part of the Rideau system, it is deep and generally free from shoals. See Chart 1513-2.

right:
Westport
Harbour

below:
Visitor
Welcome
Centre,
Westport

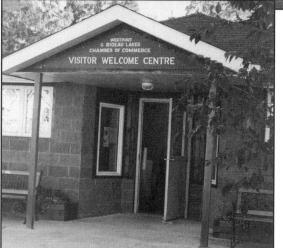

Visit the **Westport & Rideau Lakes Chamber of Commerce Visitor Welcome Centre** located on Spring Street, just up from the harbourfront between the post office and library. Washrooms with showers are available as well as an office with local brochures and an attendant who can provide information.

Westport Mill Pond

Upper Rideau Lake

Westport, Chart 1513-2

photo credit: Canadian Hydrographic Service

Westport has over 100 businesses, restaurants, stores and two nearby golf courses. With several wonderful B&Bs, cottage rentals, a motel and a country inn, you are sure to find the perfect accommodation to suit your needs. There is a post office, pharmacy, coin laundry, bank machine, large grocery store, beer and liquor store and hardware store. Excellent shopping with unique shops offer everything from gifts and one of a kind fashions to antiques and original art. There are a variety of restaurants including a piano bar, a road house and a British style pub in which to dine or relax.

Westport Harbour provides docking facilities, barbecues, and full marina services. Friendly staff are available to serve you seven days a week. Gas is available at Mansers Marina.

From May until mid-October boaters can take advantage of Westport's Municipal Dock located on Upper Rideau Lake. The village is easily accessible via a footbridge. Also within easy driving of Westport are dozens of lakes, which range in size from small to large, and which are suitable for all water related activities including canoeing and fishing.

For more information about Westport call 613-273-2929 or check the chamber of commerce web-site: www.westportrideaulakes.on.ca

view of Upper Rideau Lake, foot bridge and docking facilities from the Westport Spring

Narrows Lock:35

The Narrows Lock completed the northern end of the water summit. Originally, Upper Rideau Lake and Big Rideau Lake were one lake. Due to the arduous procedure involved in blasting through the Isthmus, By felt he could forego further excavation by raising the water level of Upper Rideau Lake. This necessitated construction of a lock at the narrows. The four-foot ten-inch raise in the lake level precluded a further four-foot ten-inch excavation at the Isthmus canal. The blockhouse, which was completed in 1833, was restored in the late 1960s. It, along with the Newboro blockhouse, was built to guard the summit of the waterway.

Due to gusty winds often present at this site, the best tie-up space is downstream from the lock where it is more sheltered. When there is a strong wind, the lockstaff will advise boaters how best to proceed into the lock. There are no stores, accommodations, or restaurants in the vicinity and the closest gas bar is four miles away in either direction.

Upper Rideau Lake

Narrows Bay
Big Rideau Lake

Narrows Lock, Chart 1513-2   *photo credit: Canadian Hydrographic Service*

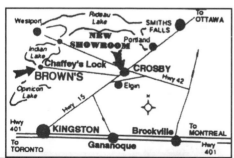

Portland

*ℒ*ocated on the east shore of Big Rideau Lake and adjacent to Hwy 15, Portland has long been a haven to travellers. First known as 'The Landing' in the 1820s, it served as a launching point for settlers bound, by barge, for Perth. This area was highly regarded for its good timberlands and arable soil. A substantial farming community was already thriving by the time the Rideau construction began. The completion of the Rideau gave Portland a boost commercially and trade became an integral part of community life. Potash, cheese and local produce were shipped to cities in exchange for tea, sugar and dry goods. The lumber trade eventually replaced Portland's potash industry. Steamboats stopped here for supplies en route from Kingston to Ottawa.

Portland has maintained its long-standing reputation as a port town. The deep waters of the Big Rideau Lake have attracted boaters for many generations, many of them owning Dowsett boats which were built locally. The Big Rideau Lake Association began in Portland in 1911 with a small group of people concerned with the preservation and safety of the lake and are today committed to long-term environmental protection and service to all who use the lake and share its resources. The large public wharf is located in the village proper where there are restaurants, a post office, shops, a bank and bank machine, medical clinic, hardware store and liquor/beer store as well as accommodations. Portland is home to the **Portland Bay B&B**, which is home base to **Rideau Canal Boat Tours**, overnight, dinner or lunch packages including cruises from Portland to Chaffey's Lock or Chaffey's to Jones Falls. For details call 613-272-0222 or visit www.bbcanada.com/portland bay

'Chuckles', Classic Rideau Cruises, Rideau Boat Tours - home base is Portland Bay B&B

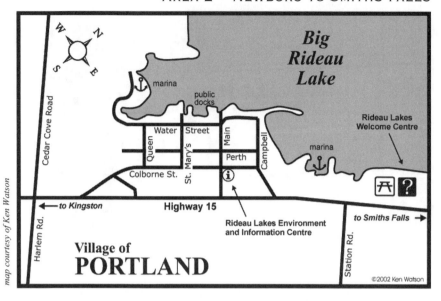

map courtesy of Ken Watson

Big Rideau Lake

marina

public docks

Cedar Cove Road

Water Street

Queen

St. Mary's

Main

Perth

Campbell

Colborne St.

Rideau Lakes Welcome Centre

marina

Harlem Rd.

← to Kingston

Highway 15

to Smiths Falls →

Station Rd.

Rideau Lakes Environment and Information Centre

Village of
PORTLAND

©2002 Ken Watson

The Galley Restaurant at Len's Cove Marina, Portland

Portland Public Wharf

Rideau Lakes Welcome Centre on Hwy #15 at Portland

There are several shops in town, groceries and more are available at Portland Foodland Food Market.

Portland has antique stores, gift and collectible shops, an art gallery, Bed and Breakfasts, restaurants, a bank and liquor store. Portland's lovely waterfront is imbued with a quiet holiday charm.The Cataraqui all-season trail passes east of town and golf courses can be found nearby. The Forfar Cheese Factory is a few kilometres south of town. Many vacationers are attracted to Portland by the excellent boating and fishing. There are several **full service marinas** in town, a variety of boat rentals and tours are also available.

Portland is conveniently located on Highway 15 between Smiths Falls and Kingston.

Portland, Chart 1513-2   *photo credit: Canadian Hydrographic Service*

Len's Cove Marina, located in the cove named for the current operator's father, offers complete marine facilities. Enjoy some great food and hospitality at **The Galley Restaurant** overlooking the water. This marine resort also offers rental cottages and a swimming pool.

Len's Cove Marina, Portland

Murphys Point Provincial Park

*L*ocated on the west side of Big Rideau Lake, this 1,240 ha (3,500 acre) park is a popular attraction for motorists and boaters alike. Murphys Point features 14 boat-in campsites, 12 of which have docking facilities for boats up to 21 feet in length (docks for overnight campers only). The remaining two campsites are canoe-in only. All boat-in sites are located in four marked clusters along the Big Rideau Lake shoreline. By car you can find the park off County Rd. 21, 19 km south of Perth.

Murphys Point lies on the Frontenac Axis, a southern extension of the Canadian Shield. The resulting rugged terrain is home to a mosaic of mature forests, lakes, wetlands, open fields, and outcrops of ancient bedrock. Hike the Point Trail (5.5 km), starting from the boat launch parking area, out to the tip of the peninsula and take a swim or picnic at the natural beach along the way. The 2.5 km Sylvan Trail and the accompanying interpretive trail booklet explore the fascinating geology and forest ecology of the park. The 1 km Loon Lake Loop Trail offers a glimpse of a typical Canadian Shield lake.

The restored McParlan House and the remnants of the Burgess Sawmill date back to c. 1810. Both are situated at the site where Black Creek empties into Hogg Bay. Due to its cultural significance, this site is now the focus of an archaeological investigation, spearheaded by the Friends of Murphys Point Park. To get there, hike the McParlan House Trail (2.5 km) or the Rideau Trail (300 km, Kingston to Ottawa), or paddle into Hogg Bay (no motorboats allowed).

Murphys Point is also rich in cultural history features. The 2.5 km Silver Queen Mine Trail starts at the Lally Homestead, which includes two restored buildings and remnants of several others that date back to the 1870s. Numbered posts along the trail correspond to stops in the interpretive booklet and explain the history of the area's mica mining industry, which flourished in the early 1900s. The mine is open during guided tours that run from July to October.

Take a guided tour of the Silver Queen Mica Mine, call 613-267-5060 for tour times and reservations.

Other facilities include a fully-stocked Park Store with canoe rentals, 2 sandy beaches, 20 km of groomed ski trail, 160 regular campsites (in addition to the 14 boat-ins), 27 with electrical service, 1 barrier-free site, and 3 group campsites that accommodate up to 150 people. Swimming, picnicking, hiking, wildlife viewing, fishing, and boating are among the activities most popular. From July to October, park naturalists conduct up to 12 free programs per week, including children's programs, guided hikes, evening slide talks, and special events. Call the park for a weekly program schedule.

The 14 boat-in campsites are reserve-able. Regular campsites can be reserved up to five months in advance by calling 1-888-ONT-PARK or by internet at www.OntarioParks.com. Due to the popularity of this park, especially over summer weekends and holidays, a reservation is recommended. Group campsite reservations can be made by calling the park directly at 613-267-5060. For more general information, visit the website or call the park.

Navigation Note: Rocky Narrows is a deep channel that joins two sections of Big Rideau Lake. Murphys Point is the NW entrance to Rocky Narrows.

Colonel By Island

$\mathcal{A}$pproximately three miles east of the Narrows Lock on Big Rideau Lake, is Colonel By Island. However, you will find it is marked as Long Island on your chart. This island, formerly a private estate, is now owned by Parks Canada and is great for overnight docking. The island has barbecues, washrooms, water, a tennis court, and an excellent unsupervised swimming area. It is a nice place to stop for a wander along the self-guiding trail and have a picnic or camp overnight. There are 336 feet of overnight mooring space and 126 feet of day use space available.

A peaceful day at the dock.

Navigation Notes: Big Rideau Lake - the SW part of the lake is 4 miles/9 kms wide, the main navigation route is along the western shore. The lake is deep and generally free of dangers. Note a shoal north of Sand Island, see Chart 1513-2. The SE portion of the lake has many islands and shoals. Portland is located at the SE corner of the lake. The route to Portland leaves the main route just NE of Sand Island.

Rideau Ferry

This small community at the junction of Big Rideau and Lower Rideau Lakes was originally known as Oliver's Ferry or Oliver's Landing. Oliver was a ferryman, as local lore tells, a number of late travellers, offered lodging at his home, were reported to have ferried across the lake in the morning but were never seen again.

Today, the hamlet of Rideau Ferry offers Rideau Ferry General Store . The Rideau Ferry Marina and Rideau Ferry Harbour offer marina services and the Shipwreck Restaurant offers docking facilities as well. The public wharf has depths of 3 to 5 feet. A number of antique shops can be found nearby. Rideau Ferry is located on County Road #1 between Lombardy and Perth and is easily reached from Hwy 15.

Nearby, visitors will find the Rideau Ferry Yacht Club Conservation Authority Beach. Washrooms and change rooms are available, the beach is unsupervised. Visitors by car will find the driveway to the Conservation Area and Beach just past the entrance to the Shipwreck Restaurant off County Road #1. A parking fee is requested and payment is by the honour system. This is a nice spot for a picnic and a swim on a hot day.

Public Wharf at Rideau Ferry

Navigation Note: Rideau Ferry is on the North shore of the narrows that connect Big Rideau Lake and Lower Rideau Lake. The entrance to Lower Rideau Lake, the last of the chain of Rideau Lakes is at Rideau Ferry. Lower Rideau Lake is the shallowest of all the Rideau Lakes - keep to the navigation channel.

Rideau Ferry from east, Chart 1513-1   *photo credit: Canadian Hydrographic Service*

Rideau Ferry from south, Chart 1513-1   *photo credit: Canadian Hydrographic Service*

Rideau Ferry from west, Chart 1513-1   *photo credit: Canadian Hydrographic Service*

Beveridges Locks: 33-34

*T*his spur route into Perth was not originally part of the Rideau. A group of Perth merchants saw the opportunity afforded to them by linking Perth with the Rideau for the purpose of trade and commerce. They formed the Tay Navigation Company in order to fund and construct the Tay Canal. Construction began in 1832 and, when completed, consisted of five detached locks, six dams and a turning basin. By the late 1800s the government had taken over this private concern and built two locks in a new canal which considerably shortened the route from Perth to Lower Rideau Lake.

Lower Rideau Lake is often very windy and many boaters duck into the Tay Canal for a short, sheltered respite from the blow. Care must be taken to stay in the channel when approaching the locks. There is ample tie-up space at the Lower Beveridges lock. Farther upstream is Upper Beveridges. During lock operating hours 240 ft of tie up space is available in between the two.

It is only 10 km (6.5 miles) from Upper Beveridges to Perth. At Perth the Last Duel Park offers 100 feet of docking facilities with wash-rooms, water, pump-out stations and power hook-ups. It is only a ten minute walk to the downtown shopping core from the park. The bridge at the park has a 7 foot clearance and most smaller craft can easily navigate through to the turning basin.

locks at Upper Beveridges Cut

Photo Credit: Kevin Fox, Rideau Canal Parks Canada

facilities at lower Beveridges

facilities at upper Beveridges

photo credit: Canadian Hydrographic Service   *Beveridges Bay, Chart 1513-1*

Navigation Notes:
1)Beveridge Bay is an open shallow bay on NW side of Lower Rideau Lake.
2)The entrance to the Tay Canal, marked by day beacons, can be difficult to see.
3)There are 4 bridges to consider on the approach to Perth, the lowest clearance is 6 feet at Beckwith Street Bridge. See Chart 1513-1.

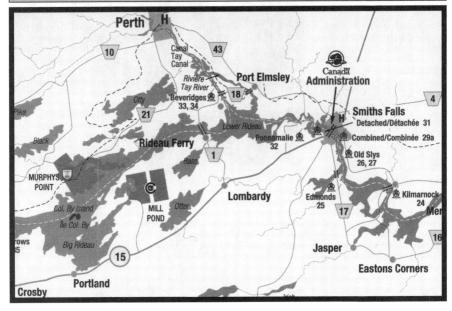

map courtesy of Parks Canada

Perth

Named after Perth, Scotland, this was originally a military settlement. After the Napoleonic Wars ended, England encouraged disbanded soldiers to emigrate to Upper Canada by giving them land grants. This first settlement at Perth was established in 1816.

Perth became a busy community but little trade was undertaken as the overland journey to Brockville was treacherous and time-consuming. It was not until the Tay Canal was completed in 1834 that Perth really began to thrive. The Tay Navigation Company, comprised of private citizens, instigated and funded the canal construction to enable Perth to gain commercial access to neighbouring settlements and larger communities such as Kingston, Montreal and Bytown.

Perth is a truly beautiful town. It has every amenity for visitors and provides a pleasant atmosphere. Most of the original homes and buildings are still standing and many of them have been restored, as a walk down the tree-lined streets of the downtown core will prove. Since many of the settlers were Scottish stonemasons, the buildings were extremely well-constructed and a walking tour is most interesting. A brochure with three self-guided walking tours can be picked up at the Visitor Information Centre at the Old Fire Hall on Herriot Street near Gore. The accompanying history makes for an educational experience as well. TRIVIA: Did you know that the last fatal duel in Canada was fought here between law students, Robert Lyon and John Wilson in 1833, over the hand of local governess, Elizabeth Hughes? This battle was fought on the banks of the Tay at what is now known as **Last Duel Park**. Lyon's tombstone can be found in the **Old Burying Grounds** close by.

Of particular interest is **Matheson House** which was built around 1840. This was the residence of Roderick Matheson, one of Canada's first senators. It is located at 11 Gore Street and houses the Perth Museum. The museum contains many pioneering artifacts including a piece of the mammoth cheese which went to the World's Fair in Chicago (1893) and also the pistols of the famed last duel.

The **Town Hall**, at 80 Gore Street, and **Victoria Hall**, at 33 Drummond Street, which is now the Great War Memorial Hospital, were built in 1863 and 1858 respectively. **Inge-va** may be viewed by appointment only, although the garden is open to the general public. It is located at 66 Craig Street. This gracious home was built in 1823 and

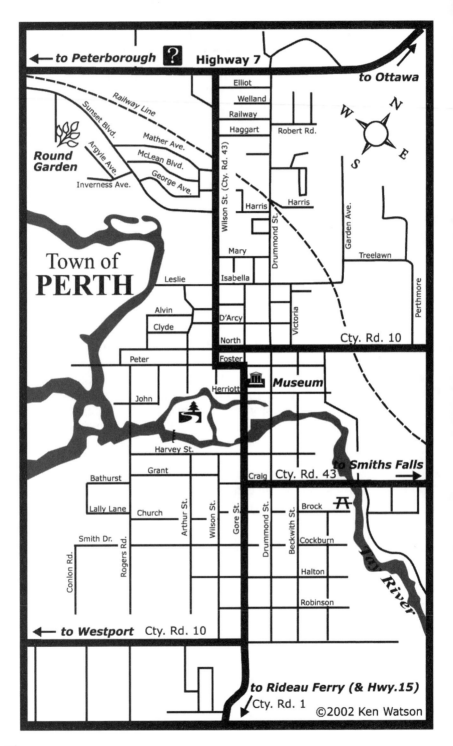

was owned at one time by Thomas Radenhurst, a lawyer and the uncle of dueler Robert Lyon. Lyon also resided and died in the house. **The Daniel McMartin House** was built in 1830 and was the home of Perth's first lawyer. This home, at 125 Gore Street, is a fine example of Federal style architecture, native to the New England States during the turn of the 19th century. Other heritage buildings of interest are **Haggart House** -1840 and **Summit House** -1823. **The Old Fire Hall** now houses the Visitor Information Centre on Herriott Street near Gore and is located next door to the **Perth Public Library**.

Stewart Park behind the Town Hall is the place to be when the Perth Citizens Band strikes up a concert every second Thursday during the summer. An evening of listening will be sure to raise your spirits. In July enjoy three days of free musical entertainment with over 20 live concerts at the **Stewart Park Festival**. The park is located on what was once McLaren's Distillery, so the area seems destined to raise spirits.

Stewart Park, Perth

In August the **Perth Garlic Festival** is a very popular attraction, as is the exciting **Glen Tay Block Race**. Information about these events and the **Central Canadian Fiddling and Stepdancing Championships** can be found at the tourist information centre located in the Old Fire Hall on Herriot Street.

Farmers Market at the Crystal Palace, Perth

photo credit: Penny Thompson

Labour Day Weekend is when the **Perth Agricultural Fair** gets underway. The fair is preceded by a large parade and the whole weekend is guaranteed fun for everyone. May thru October the Perth **Farmers Market** is open in Downtown Perth every Saturday morning. All produce is local. Enjoy the produce, baked goods, preserves, quality crafts and much more. Special themes and different events take place each Saturday. Call 613-267-4003 for details.

Apart from these special events there is plenty of theatrical entertainment for you in Perth throughout the summer. The **Perth Studio Theatre** performs award-winning, original productions for your enjoyment. Call 613-267-7469 for information.

An abundance of dining choices from fast food to gourmet cuisine can be found in Perth. Quaint shops, book stores, boutiques, groceries, hardware, pharmacies, beer and liquor stores and more are all found in this full service town. Stroll down mainstreet and browse, visit the farmers market or relax and dine at a quaint outdoor café. Be sure to stop for a while and enjoy all that Perth has to offer.

Code's Mill, home to delightful shops & restaurants, across from Stewart Park in historic Perth.

Mud Cut & Slab Island, Chart 1513-1   *photo credit: Canadian Hydrographic Service*

Navigation Note: Mud Cut is a former dredged channel suitable for boats of shallow draught, leading NE from the main route and offers small boats a short cut. Caution -submerged embankments on either side present a hazard, refer to Chart 1513-1.

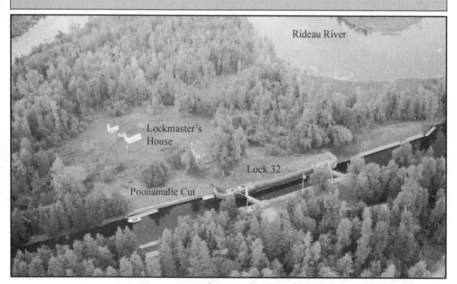

Poonamalie Lock, Chart 1513-1   *photo credit: Canadian Hydrographic Service*

Navigation Note: The section of river from Poonamalie to Smiths Falls is winding and narrow with shoals extending from both banks. Hunter Rock, 400 ft north of Bacchus Island, may be awash or submerged depending on water levels.

Poonamalie Lock:32

*F*irst Rapids, as it was originally called, encompassed a stretch of shallow rapids 200 m/650 feet long. It is speculated that its later name Poonamalie was given by one of the Royal Sappers and Miners who served in India.

By's initial plan to make the river navigable was thwarted. He had wanted to raise the water level of the river to drown the rapids but the banks were too low to sustain that. The alternate plan was to excavate the river bed, thus making it deep enough for navigation. This was also not feasible due to the hard limestone riverbed. Finally, a narrow canal was cut along the bank of the river and a lock with a lift of almost six and a half feet was built. Unmarked graves around the lock-site are those of canal workers who like so many before and after them died of malaria.

Poonamalie is a very picturesque lockstation. It is quite busy during the summer and is especially popular with road visitors. The locksite has barbecues and picnic tables. Upstream from the lock, you'll find 300 feet of tie-up space and an additional 75 feet downstream. Although there are no grocery stores or other amenities in the immediate vicinity, a general store and gas docks are available at Rideau Ferry, 10 km/6 miles away. There is a walking trail from the lockstation that is about three quarters of a mile long and leads to the control dam. It is a scenic walk and takes about fifteen minutes.

Rideau River

Poonamalie Cut

photo credit: Canadian Hydrographic Service   Poonamalie Lock, Chart 1513-1

Smiths Falls

*S*miths Falls was built on a land grant given in 1794 to Thomas Smyth, a United Empire Loyalist. James Simpson and Abel Ward, co-founders of the town, realized the commercial potential of Smiths Falls and designed the lay-out of the town with this in mind. Broad roads were built to link Smiths Falls to surrounding communities. Within a short time the village, which had a saw mill, grist mill, flour mill, blacksmith, two stores and a tannery, had developed so rapidly it surpassed both Kemptville and Merrickville as a major commercial centre. Trade, which was carried on via the Rideau, was given a further boost when the CPR ran its main rail line through the town.

Smiths Falls is a congenial town and, thanks to the foresight of its founders, has an openness many towns cannot achieve. The wide main street and numerous parks lend a spaciousness to the town. Among the many attractions for tourists is **Heritage House Museum**. In this 19th century Victorian home, eight period rooms have been carefully restored to depict an upper middle class life style in 1867-75. This home also has unique mirror-image facades and the only remaining two storey privy in Ontario. Call 613-283-8560 for hours of operation. The museum is located on Old Slys Road not far from the Old Slys Lockstation and is open year round.

About a half mile from the lockstation, is the **Hershey Chocolate Shoppe® Visitors Centre and Factory Tour.** This famous attraction welcomes visitors to its large store and elevated viewing level. Open daily year round, your family will love it.

Hershey Chocolate Shoppe®

A visit to the combined lockstation is a must in Smiths Falls. The three original manual locks were replaced in 1973 by a single hydraulic lock. The original manual locks have been preserved for public viewing and it proves interesting to compare them to the contemporary lock. On-site exhibits explain the locks and how they work.

The world class **Rideau Canal Museum** offers five floors of a unique blend of historic displays, artifacts and modern technology. The museum traces the building and evolution of this historic canal with touch screen computers, laser disc minitheatres and a "Tunnel of History". It is located at 34 Beckwith Street South. Call 613-284-0505 for information.

Discover a Canadian Northern Railway Station at the **Smiths Falls Railway Museum of Eastern Ontario**. This National Historic Site offers Wickham car rides, tours, operational equipment, demos, displays and special events. The museum is located at 90 William Street West and is open daily May through October. Call 613-283-5696 for hours of operation and special events. The Museum celebrates a **Chocolate and Railroad Festival** in July.

Keep an eye open for the **Smiths Falls Bascule Bridge National Historic Site** about 1.5 km south of the Railway Museum. This bridge, constructed in 1912-13, is the oldest surviving structure of its type in Canada. Also known as a Scherzer Rolling Lift Bridge, it is a unique attrac-

Bascule Bridge Smiths Falls

Photo Credit: Bill Pratt, Rideau Canal Parks Canada

tion and crosses the Rideau Canal just to the south of the Smiths Falls Locks. View at the Detached Lock off Abbott Street.

Smiths Falls has a great variety of **restaurants**, **shops**, **accommodations** and services for visitors as well as a number of beautiful parks. **Victoria Park**, which has overnight docking, water, power hook-ups, a wading pool, and playground, also provides camping facilities. It is a

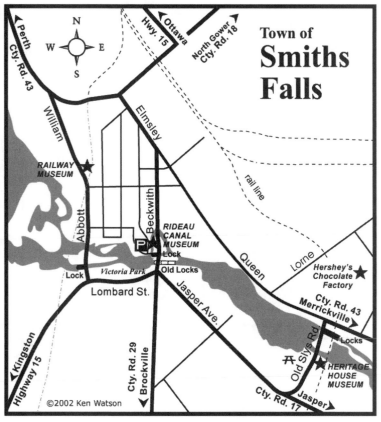

79

Centennial Park, Smiths Falls

Victoria Park Docks

perfect setting for boaters and motorists to compare notes.

Centennial Park is a bright spot in town and has beautiful floral displays and three fountains. **Hydro Park** has a sandy beach with unsupervised swimming.

Beside the flight of old locks is the **Lockmaster's House** at 1 Jasper Avenue, home to the Friends of the Rideau, a volunteer, non-profit association working in cooperation with Parks Canada. They are dedicated to enhancing and conserving the heritage and charm of the waterway.

Shop or dine in the historic downtown. B&Bs, hotels and motels will accommodate you while you take part in the many special events that take place in this historic town. Contact the Welcome Centre for an events schedule, call 1-800-257-1334 or visit www.smithsfalls.ca

Victoria Park Welcome Centre

info

Rideau River

Victoria Park

Combined Lock

Rideau Canal Museum

Old Locks

Smiths Falls from east Chart 1512-3   *photo credit: Canadian Hydrographic Service*

Smiths Falls Locks

⌐The site at Smiths Falls presented much the same geographical problem to Colonel By as Poonamalie did. Hard limestone bedrock ruled out the possibility of excavating or blasting a long channel and the lowlands around the Rideau River in this locale prevented raising the water level to flood the rapids rendering this section navigable. Instead, By decided to build two separate sets of locks, Smiths Falls Detached Lock and Smiths Falls Combined Locks.

Smiths Falls Detached Lock: 31

⌐This single lock gives an eight and a half foot drop into the Smiths Falls turning basin and offers an excellent concrete launching ramp and 2000 feet of tie-up space. It is approximately a fifteen minute walk from here to the Combined Locks and downtown shopping area.

Smiths Falls Combined Locks:
(28,29,30)29A

Below the original rapids in Smiths Falls, Colonel By decided to blast a canal cut through the jut of land around which the river curved. Three locks were built in this cut, giving a combined lift of 25 feet. Two embankments extending upstream from the canal walls retained a water level which the naturally low banks could not have supported. A dam of 23 feet and a waste weir helped maintain a good depth in the basin.

The one problem which remained unresolved was the riverbed itself. It was full of fissures, through which water seeped until 1959, when a new concrete dam was built. A new hydraulic lock, 29a, which operates today as Smiths Falls Combined Lock, was built in 1973 in a cut excavated alongside the original three combined locks. Although the original locks are officially closed, they remain intact for viewing. The locking experience here is quite different from others on the system.

Near the combined locks is Victoria Park. There is a fee for overnight docking and the facilities include hydro, water, showers, and pump-out. There is also a playground and wading pool for children.

photo credit: Canadian Hydrographic Service   *Smiths Falls from west, Chart 1513-1*

Smiths Falls to Ottawa

Boats at Merrickville
Photo Credit: Elisabeth McEuen,
Rideau Canal, Parks Canada

Area 3

Old Slys Locks:27 - 26

This lock site was named after William Sly who settled here with his family in 1798. His house and barn stood where the lockmaster's house now stands. Once again Colonel By had to rethink the original plan for these two locks. The initial plan called for an angled construction which would have shortened excavation, but when By was instructed to enlarge the lock chambers to facilitate steamboats, he had to excavate a longer channel in order to house the two locks in a conventional straight formation. The 23 foot dam presented some difficulties as well. The river flowed over the dam and since the bedrock could not bear up to the water pressure, a waste weir was built to divert excess water away from the dam and an additional three feet were added to the top of the dam to prevent overflow.

Old Slys is one minute by car from downtown Smiths Falls. It is the closest lockstation to the **Hershey Chocolate Shoppe®& Factory**, which is half a mile away. Close to the upstream lock is Lower Reach Park which has docking facilities, tennis courts and picnic area. The **Heritage House Museum** is just east of the park. Groceries and gas are available 200 feet from the lock. The nearest marina downstream is in Merrickville and upstream at Rideau Ferry.

Old Slys Locks looking SE, Chart 1512-3   *photo credit: Canadian Hydrographic Service*

Edmonds Lock:25

*T*his land was owned by James Edmonds (Edmunds) who was one of the first settlers in the area. Initially By had intended to build locks at Edmonds and Phillips Bay, but the land drop turned out to be considerably less than originally thought. Since the river banks were higher at Edmonds, it was decided to build there and construction of an overflow dam and lock were begun.

Today the locksite remains virtually unchanged. This quiet, secluded site provides no amenities and tie-up space is limited.

photo credit: Simon Lunn, Rideau Canal, Parks Canada   *Edmonds Dam*

Rideau River

Dam

Weir

lock 25

Rideau River

photo credit: Canadian Hydrographic Service   *Edmonds Lock, Chart 1513-3*

Kilmarnock Lock:24

*A*t this site, once called Maitland's Rapids, several problems were encountered. The rapids had to be flooded, but the upriver banks were too low to withstand higher waters. When canal excavation began, the riverbed proved swampy and, as at the Cataraqui sites, malaria broke out. These problems were eventually overcome by building an embankment along the naturally low banks, lowering the dam and slightly altering the canal location through rocky, rather than swampy land.

Kilmarnock is quiet. There are no stores, restaurants or accommodations in the nearby area, but the bird population is tremendous. This area is truly a bird-watcher's paradise. Downstream tie-up space is limited, but upstream there is 100 feet. A visit to the nearby apple orchard in Jasper may prove rewarding, if the season is right.

Rideau River

Lock 24

Kilmarnock Island

Rideau River

Kilmarnock　　　　　　　*photo credit: Canadian Hydrographic Service*

Bridge at Kilmarnock

Navigation Note: A bird sanctuary lies on either side of the waterway for about 2 miles/4.5 kms just west of Merrickville. Signs are posted to indicate sanctuary limits. North of the canal approach to Merrickville is a sheltered basin known locally as 'the pond'.

photo credit: Canadian Hydrographic Service

approaching Merrickville from the west, chart 1512-3

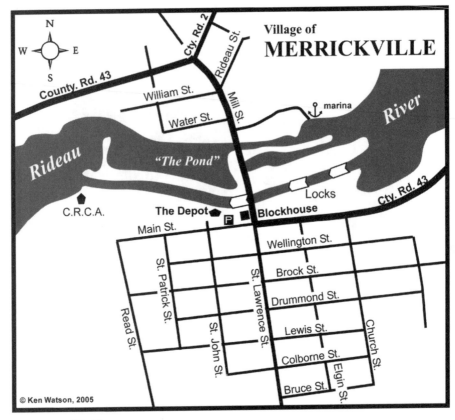

map courtesy of Ken Watson

Locking Through Merrickville

Merrickville

*I*n 1998, Merrickville was named 'Canada's Prettiest Village' by Communities in Bloom and no wonder. The sunlight sparkles on the river; trailing flowers cascade from the many hanging flower baskets along the streets, and boats of all sizes move gracefully through the locks.

Settled by William Merrick in 1794, Merrickville was once one of the largest industrial centres on the Rideau with gristmills, sawmills and woolen mills operating beside the river. When Colonel By constructed the Rideau Canal, he built three locks here. The original blockhouse, built for defense purposes, still stands beside the Canal just across the road from the Lockmaster's House.

One can gain a clearer insight into the boom of Merrickville when visiting the **Industrial Heritage Complex Museum**, located on the island at the lockstation. The museum outlines industrial progress along the Rideau.

Today Merrickville is a favourite stopping place for boaters and shoppers as well as history buffs. A visit to **'The Depot'** operated by the Friends of the Rideau is a must for information and history on the canal. Located on the waterfront adjacent to the Blockhouse, it is the retail outlet and interpretive centre for the 'Friends'. It is open daily from mid-June to the end of September. Rideau souvenirs can be found here.

The *Depot to Dam* trail takes visitors from the Friends of the Rideau retail outlet and interpretive centre, The Depot, to the tip of the old cut stone dam at the west end of the embankment

The Depot

The Harriet By Electric Tour Boat at The Depot

that separates the original channel of the Rideau River from the artificial canal cut. The trail heads out along this embankment and provides the visitor with interesting views of heritage and nature. The interpretive brochure, available at *The Depot*, not only guides your way but informs and delights.

Tours aboard the Harriet By, an electric tour boat, will take you for an up close look at the local Bird Sanctuary. Tour schedules and tickets are available at *The Depot*.

Merrickville is also home to the **Canadian Recreational Canoeing Association Headquarters**, located at the *Rideau Outdoor Centre* in the nearby Merrickville Fairgrounds. Check out the Rideau by Paddle section for more details about this organization.

For overnight accommodation, there are two inns and several bed and breakfasts located in the village. Almost every amenity is within walking distance from the locks: supermarket, bank, liquor store, gas stations, shops, restaurants and accommodation.

There are many restaurants and eating places in the village. You can choose casual food such as pizza or English pub fare at the **Goose & Gridiron**, the light menu of a café or the full course menus of several fine dining establishments, including **Sam Jakes Inn and the Baldachin Inn**. Dress is generally casual. You must drop in at '**Round the Corner Bakeshop** for some freshly baked bread or a delicious pastry.

Mirick's Landing Country Store, corner of St. Lawrence and Main Streets

In early July is **Merrickville Canalfest**, a celebration of the Rideau Canal including demonstrations, canoe races, shows, theatre, music, BBQs and fun events. The **Merrickville Agricultural Fair and Steamshow** is usually the second weekend of August. Later in August is the **Canadian Canoe Symposium** hosted by the Canadian Recreational Canoe Association at the Rideau Outdoor Centre. The **Annual Classic Antique and Collectible Show** is in late August. The **Merrickville Artists Studio Tour and Sale** takes place the last weekend of September and first weekend of October.

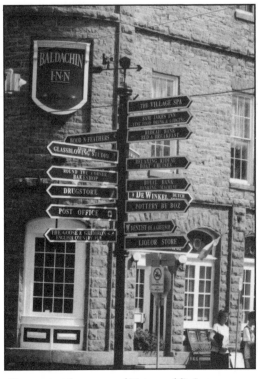

Sign post at the corner of Main and St. Lawrence Streets across from the Baldachin Inn, offering fine dining, accommodations, boutique and pub in a 1860 heritage building, once the largest department store between Chicago and Montreal.

Merrickville from south, Chart 1512-3   *photo credit: Canadian Hydrographic Service*

Shopping ~ Dining ~ Accommodation.....
Merrickville has it all!

Merrickville is home to 50 quaint boutiques, galleries, artist studios and specialty food and gift shops. From glass blowing to pottery to handcrafted leather goods, you'll find all you could ask for here. Visitors travel from far and wide to spend a day or two shopping or browsing in Merrickville. Most of the shops are housed in heritage buildings adding to the delightful atmosphere of the town. All the shops, on the main streets or the side streets are within easy walking distance from the lockstation, a parking lot on the main street will accommodate all visitors. Whatever your taste or budget, you're sure to find something that pleases in Merrickville.

You'll need more than a day to take it all in and you certainly won't go hungry with over a dozen eating establishments to choose from, you'll want to try more than one. For more information about where to eat, shop or stay in Merrickville, go to the Chamber of Commerce website at www.realmerrickville.ca or call 613-269-2229.

Sam Jakes Inn, Main Street, Merrickville

SamJakes
• Inn •

&

The Village Spa

**Experience Historic Merrickville
while staying at the heritage
Sam Jakes Inn.
Choose from a variety of
overnight packages.**

◆◆◆◆◆◆◆◆◆◆◆◆◆◆◆◆◆◆◆◆◆◆◆◆◆◆◆◆◆

**118 Main St. E. Box 580
Merrickville, On K0G 1N0
613-269-3711 or 1-800-567-4667**
www.samjakesinn.com

Merrickville Locks:23-22-21

The largest of the four blockhouses on the Rideau was built at lock 21. It was a strategic place because the road from Merrick Mills to Brockville provided easy access for raiders. During the rebellion of 1837 and again in 1846 when the Oregon Crisis threatened to start a war between the Americans and Canadians, the blockhouse at Merrickville was in a constant state of readiness. It was capable of accommodating fifty soldiers.

The Blockhouse is now a museum which is open to the public during the summer. It is operated by the Merrickville Historical Society.

Average lock-through time here is about one hour. The tie-up facilities upstream of the locks are excellent, but downstream there is only blue line tie-up. The locks are in the village and are easy walking distance to all amenities.

Blockhouse Museum

photo credit: Canadian Hydrographic Service

Merrickville Chart 1512-3

View of canal from Main Street Bridge, Merrickville

Navigation Note: The railroad bridge crossing the channel just NE of Merrickville has a clearance of 39 feet/12m. The 5 mile/11km stretch of river from Merrickville locks to Burritt's Rapids is mainly uncomplicated. The channel is well buoyed. Stay within channel markers, particularly near Clowes and Andrewsville dams and rapids.

Clowes Lock from west, Chart 1512-3   *photo credit: Canadian Hydrographic Service*

Clowes Lock:20

James Clowes was a settler in this area who became involved in Rideau construction. After being contracted, he not only cleared the land at the intended locksites, but also started quarrying limestone for construction of the dams and canal walls. Unfortunately Mr. Clowes did not have the gift for construction and was eventually replaced by Alexander Hays. A single lock with a 9 1/2 foot lift was built and a 300 foot overflow dam and waste weir completed the canal works at Clowes.

There are no groceries or accommodations available in the immediate vicinity and tie-up space is limited, but it is a pleasant stop for a picnic or BBQ.

photo credit: Canadian Hydrographic Service   *Clowes Lock, Chart 1512-3*

Navigation Note: There is a strong current at the lower end of Clowes lock when water is being discharged, so boaters should be careful when approaching the blue line. Also take care on windy days, as the wind current rebounds from the high embankment on the west side of the lock.

Nicholsons Locks:19-18

$\mathcal{R}$obert Nicholson was a United Empire Loyalist who settled here about three miles upstream from Burritt's Rapids. Due to inaccurate surveying of this site, Colonel By had to re-structure the original plans. This happened so often that By must have grown to expect these foibles. Instead of flooding Nicholsons Rapids, a lower dam was built upstream. A canal, to accommodate two locks, was constructed alongside the river. Many of the Sappers and Miners working at Nicholson's Locks built their residences along the river here. Because the river was the main mode of transportation, these houses faced the water.

Nearby, a small village called Andrewsville grew around miller Rufus Andrew's flour mill. Today it is a partial ghost town and is a five minute walk from the lock. The large picnic area at Nicholson's is a popular stop for motorists. There is 120 feet or 37 metres of blueline available between upper and lower Nicholsons only during lock operating hours. An exhibit stands beside the lock office.

Nicholsons Locks, Chart 1512-3   *photo credit: Canadian Hydrographic Service*

Navigational Notes: 1)On approach to Nicholsons from the north take care to avoid the shallows on each side of the entrance.
2)The route north of Nicholsons is winding but clear.
3)Boaters are cautioned about an open dam at 1 km/.5mile SW of Burritts Rapids, the channel is clearly marked.

Rideau Canal, Parks Canada Archive

Swing Bridge at Nicholsons

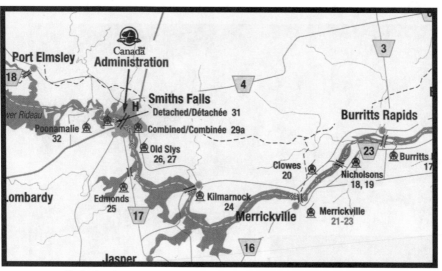

map courtesy of Parks Canada

Burritt's Rapids Lock:17

$\mathcal{J}$n 1793, United Empire Loyalists, Stephen and Daniel Burritt, made their homes here. By 1826, Stephen Burritt had built a sawmill, bridge and school near the rapids and within a few years, a small village had developed on the opposite side of the river.

Just prior to canal construction, Stephen Burritt donated land to the village on which Christ Church was built. The Christ Church, which is still in use as an Anglican church, has "bull's eye" windows which are rather unique in this part of Canada. In 1839 Burritt's Rapids was the first village in the area to have a post office. This village was a hive of activity until it, too, was bypassed by the railway and started winding down to become the quiet hamlet it now is.

When Colonel By found the lowlands here incapable of sustaining the dam and flood method to drown the rapids, he bypassed them. The lockstation is located on the island which was created from cutting the circumventing canal. A trail runs from one end of the island to the other and is aptly named **Tip to Tip Trail**. The return trip takes about two hours and will give you a chance to stretch your legs as you pass through woodland and marshes abounding with wildlife. A tour brochure is available at the lockstation. It will also give you a chance

Burritt's Rapids   *Rideau Canal, Parks Canada*

to stroll by historic homes in the village.

There is a small picnic park area at the Burritt's Rapids swing bridge in the village of Burritt's Rapids, where the Tip to Tip Trail resumes. The last weekend in July is the usual date of the Around-the-Island Canoe Race and community picnic.

There is excellent tie-up space here at the floating docks in the river channel. Burritt's Inlet offers good anchorage and swimming. **Michael's Restaurant** is equipped with many boater amenities, including a laundromat and is located at the Burritt's Rapids Lock. A **general store** can be found across the swing bridge on the village main street. The closest marina is ten miles downstream.

photo credit: Canadian Hydrographic Service

Burritt's Rapids, Chart 1512-3

Navigation Channel

Lock 17

Rideau River

Navigation Note: Boaters are cautioned to avoid an isolated shoal which is located in mid-channel immediately north east of Burritt's Rapids Lock. This shoal is marked by a spar buoy as shown on the chart.

The Long Reach

The tranquil 25 mile/40 km stretch located between the villages of Burritt's Rapids and Manotick is known as the 'Long Reach'. This is the longest lock-free stretch on the Rideau Canal system. It is a pleasant, tranquil ride through pine forests, wetlands, working farms and estate homes. Deer are often spotted grazing on the shore, blue heron and ducks dabble in the reeds and osprey are finding their homes here due to nesting platforms.

This particular area offers something for everyone: boating, swimming, fishing, camping, hiking, birding and more. The Long Reach Association, a group of local businesses, welcomes you. For more information write them at Box 41, Kars, ON, K0A 2E0 or visit their web-site: www.rideau-info.com/longreach/

view of Long Reach from Burritt's Rapids Lock

Beckett's Landing

On the way to Beckett's Landing, about 3 miles downstream from Burritt's Rapids, boaters can opt to take a detour around "The Catchall". Here you'll find a quiet, pretty spot offering good sheltered anchorage.

It is a peaceful 5 km/8 mile stretch between Burritt's Rapids and the bridge east of Beckett's Landing. You will pass historic farmsteads, Loyalist graveyards and working farms. Libby Island has a public park at the east end which is accessed from River Road. Anchorage in about 6 feet of water is possible around the southern tip of the Island.

Many local residents still carry the Beckett name and are direct decedents of the Beckett family, who settled here. A popular fishing spot is located at the bridge abutments on the south shore upstream from buoy N172.

photo credit: Elisabeth McEuen, Rideau Canal, Parks Canada   *Cruising*

Kemptville Creek, Chart 1512-2   *photo credit: Canadian Hydrographic Service*

Navigation Note: Kemptville creek is navigable by shallow draught boats for 3 miles/5 kms to the town of Kemptville. Limiting depths are 3 feet but local boaters report depths of from 7-15 ft. Boaters who intend to enter the channel must do so at right angles, do not cut this corner as a rock awash on starboard side off the point should be noted and avoided.

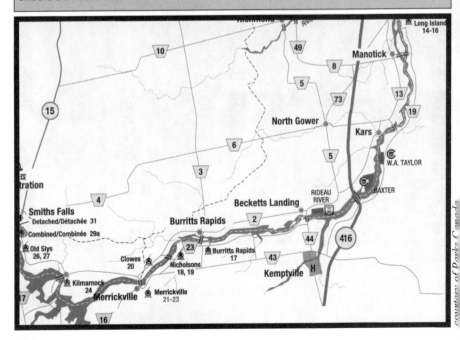

Kemptville

$\mathcal{K}$emptville was originally known as Clothiers Mill when founded in 1816. It developed as a lumber town and was changed to Kemptville in honour of Sir James Kemp, then Governor General of Upper Canada. Steamers en route from Ottawa to Montreal stopped here.

There is a public dock in town and launch ramp at Currie Park on the west side, between Bridge Street bridge and town. Bridge clearance is 11 ft/3.5 m. In town is the College of Agriculture (a campus of the University of Guelph) offering tours. The Ferguson Forest Station, borders the entire west shore from the main channel to County Road 43. Here you will find 5 miles/8 kms of hiking trails through pine forests, marshland and beech stands. A number of stores and restaurants are available. Food, hardware, liquor store, a pharmacy, gas station and medical services can be found. Tie up at the Kemptville town dock. Remember to check bridge clearance and water levels before navigating Kemptville Creek.

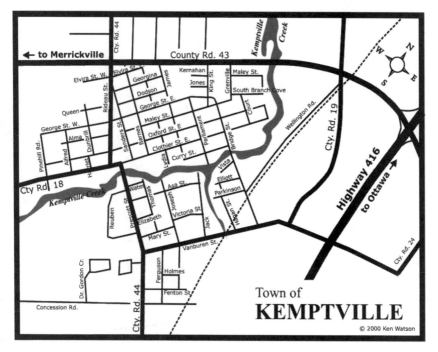

Town of
KEMPTVILLE

© 2000 Ken Watson

Rideau River Provincial Park

$\mathcal{R}$ unning for some 2.3 km along the waterway, the reforested farmland was consolidated as a park in 1959. Silver maples and pines predominate.

Located on the west bank of the Rideau River about 5 km/3 miles north of Kemptville, this park is mainly a recreational and camping area. Docking facilities in the park provide access for a variety of boats including outboards, canoes, rowboats and paddleboats. There is a wharf, for smaller boats under 16 ft, about 1/3 mile north-east of Beckett's Landing which belongs to the park, but boaters should proceed with caution because water depths are uncertain.

The park itself is very popular for day use because it has good beaches and excellent picnic facilities. Children will find hours of amusement at one of the playgrounds in the park. The network of park roads, shaded by tall pines are perfect for a family hike. A leisurely stroll along the shore could reward you with the sight of a magnificent great blue heron, American bittern, red-winged blackbird or a family of ducks paddling by, not to mention the frogs and turtles. Of the 186 campsites, 46 of them have electricity and there are two comfort stations with showers and vault toilets are easily accessible. Six group camping stations are available for 75 to 125 people.

Other park features include four sandy beaches, playgrounds and picnic areas. Fitness enthusiasts can challenge themselves on the one kilometre fitness trail featuring 10 exercise stations. There is also a golf course here, which is open to the public, as well as horseback riding. For campsite reservations or further information, phone (613) 258-2740. By car Rideau River Provincial Park can be found on regional road 13, 5 km north of Kemptville.

*photo credit:Parks Canada,
Rideau Canal*

Baxter Conservation Area

This conservation area contains 68 hectares of Parkland. Five kilometres of trails through wetlands, conifer plantations, mixed forest, nut groves and a solar energy display are offered. Picnic tables and BBQs, sandy beach and change huts, marsh boardwalk, self-guided trails and more can be enjoyed here. The Solar Energy Trail will teach you how to turn sunlight into electricity. The Filmore R. Park Nut Grove has 30 nut and bean bearing trees and Baxter Community Wildflower Garden will make your visit unforgettable. Bring your camera. It is located between Manotick and Kemptville off Hwy 416 to Dilworth Rd. For more information call 1-800-267-3504.

W. A. Taylor Conservation Area

This conservation area is located on Regional Road 19 near Osgoode. It is a great spot for a quiet picnic. A boat launch and washroom facilities are available. Taylor is the sight of some local fishing tournaments and reputed fishing hotspots are close by. Bass, perch, pickerel, panfish and even musky can be caught. Catch and release is encouraged. For information about this and other conservation areas along the Rideau call 1-800-267-3504.

Village of Kars

⁊his quaint little village, originally known as Wellington, is located on the west bank of the river. An interesting historical fact is that wood from Kars was used to build furniture on the Titanic.

There is a general store and gas station in the village, as well as a post office. Kars is inundated with visitors every year during the Kars Fair, the third week in July, when it hosts an internationally accredited dog show. This event attracts thousands of entrants from across North America. It is held in the Kars R.A. grounds and is within easy walking distance from the dock. There is plenty of parking there as well.

The public dock at Kars has docking space with depths of seven feet. There is an excellent concrete launching ramp alongside. Steven's Creek is accessible by shallow draught boats with minimum overhead clearance and leads to the Recreation Association grounds and a restaurant.

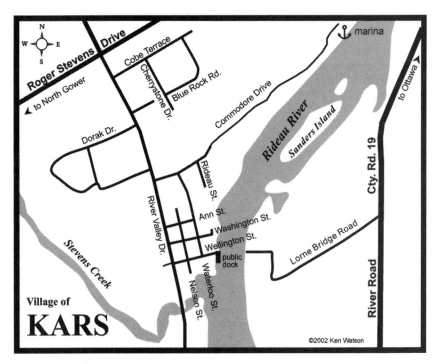

map courtesy of Ken Watson

Navigation Note: Beware of the *Cruiser Cracker* - a rock awash in the vicinity of N106. Steven's Creek is accessible to shallow draught boats with min. overhead clearance.

photo credit: Canadian Hydrographic Service

Kars, Chart 1512-2

View of Rideau River from Rideau River Provincial Park

Between Kars and Manotick on the south shore of the Rideau River, Hurst Marina and neigbouring Swan on the Rideau Restaurant stand side by side in a resort-like setting welcoming travellers arriving by boat, road or bike path.

The Swan on the Rideau, a tudor style pip of a pub transports you to merry old England with its leaded windows, beamed ceilings and cozy feel. A great spot for lunch and dinner with pub pizzazz weekdays and a hearty brunch on weekends. A crackling fireplace warms and soothes all winter long while an outdoor patio overlooking Hurst Marina and the Rideau invites and entertains all summer long.

The Swan on the Rideau Restaurant and Pub. Located next door to Hurst Marina at the Kars Bridge.

Hurst Marina, a mainstay on the Rideau for 25 years offers quality service and fine facilities. All of your boating needs can be met here: boat sales, rentals, repairs and service, mobile service and transport up to 40 feet, 30,000 lb lift as well as a full marina facility.

Hurst Marina, Manotick

Plan to stop here for an overnight stay to relax and rest up for the next days journey or stay and play. If you love boats you'll want to take in Hurst's showroom, the biggest between Toronto and Montreal. The marina offers a heated swimming pool/hot tub, clubhouse, sunbathing deck, BBQs, laundry, showers, washrooms along with the opportunity to visit the friendly Swan next door!

Manotick

𝒯he village is located on the west bank of the Rideau adjacent to
Long Island. Its name is derived from the Ojibwa word 'manot-
ic' meaning, "Island in the River". The original community in this area
began downstream near the Long Island Locks when canal workers,
who were impressed by arable land, settled there. It was not until the
1860s, that Moss Dickinson's sawmill and grist mill attracted many
mill workers upstream to this site. Dickinson, the founder of
Manotick, and his family eventually moved to Manotick where they
resided in a house built at Dickinson and Mill Streets. Manotick is
proud of its heritage and has successfully preserved it. Dickinson
Square can be found in the heart of Manotick Village. This historic
location highlights Watson's Mill, a 19th Century gristmill. This mill
is open to visitors and is still in working condition. Guided tours are
available but beware of the ghost. It is all part of the Dickinson
Square Conservation Area operated by the Rideau Valley
Conservation Authority. The house located across from the mill originally belonged to Moss Dickinson and is now a tourist attraction.

Take a walking tour and discover the village craft market, an array of
beautiful homes and delightful artists' studios. The Miller's Oven is a

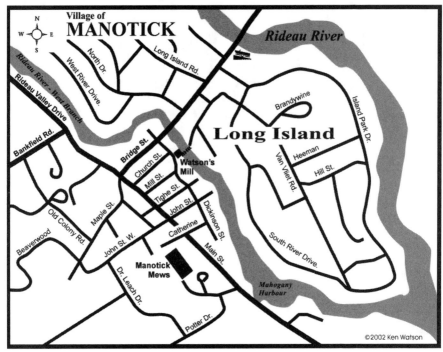

Watson's Mill

lovely tea room and bakery, which is run by seniors, it is reported to offer **'the best pie on the Rideau'**. For information about the Dickinson Square Conservation area call 1-800-267-3504.

Navigation Note: Shallow draught boats can reach **Mahogany Harbour** by turning west at buoy N90. Here you will find yourself beneath a canopy of trees. This channel will lead you to Manotick Village and Mahogany Harbour. Stay centre channel all the way and show no wake. The town float will allow you access to village amenities. Just a three minute walk will bring you to shops, restaurants, galleries and artists' studios and historic Watson's Mill. At Mahogany Harbour avoid the shoal at the entrance to the channel.

Manotick, Chart 1512-2   *photo credit: Canadian Hydrographic Service*

Manotick has managed to combine the best of both worlds. The beautiful old homes on the west side of the river and small businesses of the village proper bespeak an elegance of bygone days, while the new housing developments on the island attest to its up-to-date attitude. Over 100 stores and restaurants offer supplies, and remember this is the last stop to pick up necessities before Ottawa. Historic sites, churches, liquor and beer stores, banks, post office, public library, golf courses and tennis all make a stop in Manotick worthwhile. Contact Manotick BIA 613-692-7657 for information.

There is a Public Wharf with a draught of 5 feet located under the Bridge Street bridge. Tie up is possible and nearby one can find a launch ramp, pool, library, bait and tackle shop, medical centre and shopping plaza. Shallow draught boats can opt to tie up at the town float in Mahogany Harbour.

In Manotick summer events include the **Dickinson Days** at the beginning of June. Manotick Marina is often host to the Annual Ottawa International Antique and Classic Boat Show. Full service marina facilities are available at Manotick Marina. While docked here take a walk up the road to Millers Berry Farm and stock up on seasonal fruits and veggies. Shop for quilts and collectibles in their gift shop.

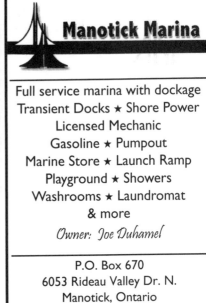

Long Island Locks:16-15-14

ecause the shallow rapids on either side of Long Island had water depths of only six inches at times, this stretch of the Rideau was not navigable before canal construction. Colonel By built a dam at the foot of the rapids which flooded them and created a slackwater from here to Burritt's Rapids. A smaller embankment was built across Mud Creek and three locks were built in the canal cut on the east side of the river. In doing so, By saved himself and his men over sixty percent of the excavation originally estimated by surveyor, Samuel Clowes. Clowes had suggested completely circumventing the rapids. During construction a village grew up at Long Island, but its demise came about as settlers were attracted to the mills of Manotick one mile away. The dam located here is the second largest stone-faced dam on the Rideau.

There is plenty of tie-up space at Long Island Locks. Apart from the 100 feet of floating wharf downstream, there is also a large bay upstream which is suitable for anchoring. A large camping area and picnic facilities are provided for boaters. The nearest stores and restaurants are at Manotick. Gas is available upstream at **Hurst Marina**. By road you will find this lockstation on River Road, 1 km west off county road 19.

photo credit: Bill Pratt, Rideau Canal, Parks Canada   *Long Island Locks, Chart 1512-2*

Black Rapids Lock, Chart 1512-1   *photo credit: Canadian Hydrographic Service*

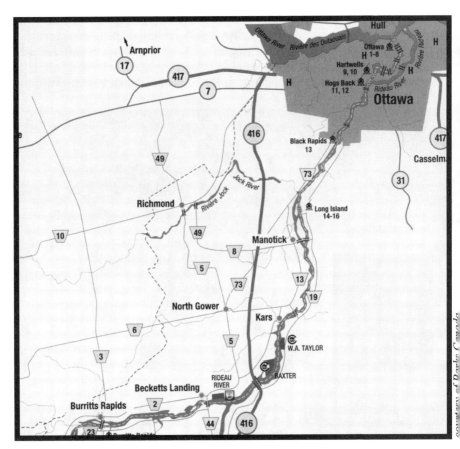

Black Rapids Lock:13

Although the river here was very wide, it was so rocky and shallow that during the summer months this four mile stretch usually had to be portaged. The 13 foot high overflow dam, which By had constructed, could not withstand the pressure of spring run-off. The water pressure eroded the bedrock dismantling the dam base and it was feared the dam structure would eventually be undermined. By's alternate measure was to become his standard dam procedure. He raised the height of the dam to prevent overflow and channeled off excess water via weirs to waste water channels. Sometimes natural creeks and snyes were used to divert waste water.

Black Rapids is the last rural lock before Ottawa. It is a very popular picnic spot with road and boat traffic. There is approximately 300 feet of tie-up space upstream from the lock and blueline tie-up downstream. Although there are no grocery stores nearby, there are restaurants and overnight accommodations within a fifteen minute walk.

Rideau Canal, Parks Canada Archive   *Black Rapids dam spans 400 ft/122 m across*

Navigation Note: Channel to the North of Black Rapids Lock is narrower and more winding between steep wooded banks, careful navigation is required.

Hogs Back Lock: 12 - 11

*L*ocal history tells that Hogs Back was named by the early settlers who likened the spiny rapids to the bony backs of wild hogs. The river at Hogs Back was over 150 feet wide and By's plan was to flood the rapids by building a 45 foot high dam. Perseverance became the 'by-word' in this construction. The project was first contracted to Walter Fenelon who, as it turned out, was inexperienced at masonry work. As he neared completion of the dam, turbulent spring flood waters washed away part of his efforts. The Royal Sappers and Miners were called in to bridge the gaping hole with timber crib and had no better luck. A flood the following year destroyed their work. Finally, it was decided to construct a timber crib across the entire width of the river. It was built to a height of 49 feet to prevent overflow and a waste weir was made to keep flood waters under control. Two locks were built in the canal, excavated between Dows Lake and the river. The downstream lock has a lift of 13 1/2 feet and the upstream lock has no lift, serving only as a guard lock to protect Lock 11 from the ravages of spring flood waters.

An interpretive trail, one mile long, runs from the lockstation to the dam. The lookout points along the trail provide an excellent view of the falls. There is blue line tie-up downstream from the locks and only limited tie-up space available on the upstream side. There are no overnight accommodations in the immediate area, but there are two shopping centres with restaurants a short walk from the lock station.

aerial view of Hogs Back Locks

photo courtesy of Ken Watson

Hartwells Locks:10 - 9

*T*hese locks were built on the man-made canal which began at the flight locks in Ottawa and eventually joined the Rideau River again at Hogs Back. The setting of these two locks is very different now from what it was during canal construction. Dows Lake was then known as Dows Great Swamp. Abraham Dow was an early settler who lived here. After the canal cuts were made and embankments built on either side of the swamp, the swamp flooded and became Dows Lake. Mooney's Bay was also a creation of the dam and flood process. Found here is another defensible lockmaster's house, however, a second storey has been added, thereby masking its military characteristics. Today, this quiet lockstation is surrounded by beautiful parkland. The Experimental Farm borders the lockstation and is a superb area for walking and learning. This farm in the city is open to the public and can provide you with an informative and pleasant day's outing. Carleton University, which is a short walk from the lock, offers bed and breakfast facilities to visitors during the summer. There is good tie-up space at the small basin upstream from the lock.

photo credit: Steve Weir, Rideau Canal Parks Canada   *Hartwells*

If the crew is looking for a bit more excitement, it's just a short cruise into Dows Lake and **Dows Lake Pavilion** and Marina. Aside from good docking, the Pavilion offers two great restaurants with waterside patios over looking the lake, including **Malone's Lakeside Bar & Grill** for a bit of languishing before heading out to explore all the sights and sounds this spectacular city has to offer. Also there's a canoe, kayak and pedal boat rental centre as part of the complex to keep the younger crew entertained. Looking north from the Pavilion across Carling Avenue see the welcoming gateway inviting visitors to explore Ottawa's "Little Italy" community with its many unique shops and restaurants. Try the renowned Pizza at a landmark watering hole, Prescott Hotel. While in the city consider using the Dows Lake Pavilion and Marina as a home base to explore Ottawa. From here it's just a short tour bus or cab ride or cycle into the heart of the nation's capital. While boaters can tie up in full view of Parliament Hill, canal wall space right in the immediate core is sometimes limited. There are no boater facilities along the wall if these are needed for overnight docking. This is not to discourage this docking option as it's a fun spot to be within walking distance of Rideau Centre, Sparks Street Mall and the ByWard Market areas all with their unique brand of shopping, touring, cultural and dining options.

Ottawa

$\mathcal{A}$s early as 1613, French Explorer Samuel de Champlain viewed this area as a good site to establish a base for his missions. He developed a good internal fur trade system with the native people.

The first permanent settler in the area was Philemon Wright who arrived in 1800 from New England to make his home in what is now Gatineau. A few years later Nicholas Sparks settled nearby on a tract of land that is now downtown Ottawa, Sparks Street is named for him. As the lumbering trade grew, more and more settlers were attracted to the area.

When Lt. Colonel By and the Royal Engineers were commissioned to construct an alternate water route through the interior, allowing the British to avoid attack by American boats on the St. Lawrence, he established base at what is now Ottawa. As construction of the Rideau Canal began, tradesmen and settlers were attracted to the area. The timber trade provided jobs for many, as did the fur trade which was still thriving. For a time, the community had a colourful reputation as a rowdy place where lumbermen converged to revel after risking life and limb in the bush. As more and more tradesmen arrived to establish themselves, the community grew and eventually became known as Bytown.

In 1854, Bytown's name was changed to Ottawa after the Outaouais Indians, an Algonquin speaking people. By this time, many lumber mills were flourishing along the waterway and the town was quite prosperous. Much to the chagrin of those in Toronto, Kingston and Montreal, seeking Capitalship for their cities, Ottawa was chosen the Capital of the Province of Canada by Queen Victoria in 1857, in spite of its rowdy reputation. In 1867, Ottawa became the National Capital, as the Province became the Dominion of Canada.

Today, bilingual Ottawa boasts qualities which are rare in large modern cities. One of these rarities is clean air. Because the Government is the largest employer in town, the high-tech industry too, there is comparatively little industrialization, hence a low pollution index. Another unusual feature is that Ottawa proper is surrounded by a greenbelt. The National Capital Commission, which was created for the purpose of beautifying the capital and preserving its endearing qualities, obtained this land to discourage urban sprawl.

The parklands bordering the Rideau Canal provide miles of pleasant walking, jogging, and biking trails. During the winter the canal is transformed into the world's longest skating rink.

During the spring, Ottawa is a blaze of colour from the thousands of tulips, a gift from Queen Juliana of Holland in return for giving her family refuge during World War II. The Annual **Canadian Tulip Festival** is an event not to be missed. During the summer, boats can tie-up right in the heart of the city. Every season reveals a new and exciting side of Canada's Capital. There is so much to see and do in Ottawa, you will need at least a few days to take it all in.

photo courtesy of the Canadian Tulip Festival

Be sure to first visit the **Capital Info Centre** across from Parliament Hill at 90 Wellington Street for all kinds of information, including a city map. Another source for info is the Capital Call Centre offering information 7 days a week at 1-800-465-1867 or 613-239-5000.

The **ByWard Market**, established by Lt.-Col. John By in 1826, is one of Canada's oldest and largest public markets, nestled in Ottawa's historic neighbourhood of Lowertown. The legendary builder of the Rideau Canal, Colonel By himself laid out the street plan of the Market, designating George Street and York Street to be extra wide to accommodate the horse drawn carriages that brought foodstuffs to market each day. The City of Ottawa has managed the outdoor market almost from the beginning - in fact, it was one of the first services provided by the municipality, ensuring a link between rural and urban life that continues into the 21st century. Today, the fun never stops at ByWard! Whether you are there at dawn to welcome the outdoor vendors, with their overflowing stands of fresh fruit and vegetables, flowers and arts & crafts or meandering through charming streets filled with eclectic boutiques and cafés, or staying up till the wee hours at one of the hit nightspots, you'll find the ByWard Market has something for you.

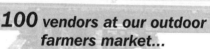

Although you might first like to tour Ottawa on a sightseeing, double decker bus to get an overall picture of the city, it is truly a walking city. It is worthwhile to sight-see some of the following on foot as they are all nestled close to each other, downtown or in the ByWard Market area.

Tour 1

Parliament Hill   *Rideau Canal, Parks Canada Archive*

A trip to Ottawa would not be complete without a visit to **The Parliament Buildings**. Located at Parliament Hill next to the flight locks, they were built between 1859 and 1865. The centre building, which was rebuilt in 1916 after a fire, is topped by the Peace Tower. The tower, which is 286 feet high, commemorates Canada's contribution to World War I. There are tours daily through the Parliament Buildings. The white light at the top of the flag pole is lit when the House of Commons is in session. It is here that you may witness the Changing of the Guard at 10:00a.m. The bright uniforms and bearskin busbies of the guards are vintage 1880 and the ceremony includes dress weaponry inspection as well as parading the colours. An Info-Tent is located between the Centre and West Blocks where tickets can be purchased for tours and refreshments and washrooms can be found. For information call 1-800-465-1867.

Then you might want to head west on Wellington to Kent Street and the **Supreme Court of Canada**, the lobby and courtroom are open to the public, admission is free. Then it is on to the **National Library and National Archives**. Located at 395 Wellington, the library is open daily. It houses Canada's history from written records and photographs to artwork and maps. Across the street is the **Garden of the Provinces**, at Wellington and Bay. This is a street corridor displaying the flag, coat of arms, and flower of each of Canada's provinces and territories. The tree fountain is quite a sight, especially at night when it is illuminated.

Rideau Canal, downtown Ottawa

Gatineau, Quebec

Parliament Hill

Ottawa River

Downtown Ottawa

Rideau Canal

photo credit: Canadian Hydrographic Service

From here, head east on Sparks to the **Sparks Street Mall**. This outdoor pedestrian mall, which continues from Kent Street to Elgin Street, is closed to traffic and contains many boutiques, stores, restaurants, outdoor bistros, fountains, and sidewalk art displays. It affords an excellent opportunity to buy souvenirs, have an afternoon snack and soak up the atmosphere. You will find the **National War Memorial**, at Confederation Square as you emerge from the Sparks Street Mall. It was originally designed to commemorate Canadians who died in World War I and now honours all of Canada's war dead.

Right across the street is the **National Arts Centre**. This is the home of the performing arts in Ottawa, where you will enjoy concerts, dramatic productions, opera, symphony, the ballet, and more in both official languages. During the summer, the terraced area around this modern and beautifully designed complex is alive with local artisans and entertainers. If you wish to view the theatre, tours are available. Enjoy Canal side dining at Le Café within the Centre, a great place for lunch, and while there check out the box office and pick up some tickets for a show. Call 613-947-7000 or TicketMaster at 613-755-1111.

From here it's a quick walk across the bridge to the **Rideau Centre** if shopping is on your mind and then on to the **ByWard Market**, the original market place of Bytown, in operation since the 1820s. Here

you will find fruits and vegetables, artisans, street performers, fresh flowers and great food in abundance. Much of the local nightlife can be found in this part of town too.

If not in the mood to shop and browse, head across Wellington to the famous **Fairmont Chateau Laurier** where you will find the **Museum of Photography** at 1 Rideau Canal between the Hotel and the Flight Locks. Here you will find displayed the work of Canada's most dynamic photographers.

Cross over to the staircase that will lead down to the Flight Locks and you find yourself at the **Bytown Museum**. If you have already travelled or are planning to travel the system you must stop here. This was the Commissariat storehouse during canal construction and now houses artifacts and exhibits pertaining to the canal and early Bytown history. The admission fee is minimal. If not visiting by boat, this is a good time to watch the boats lock through, an incredible sight, particularly here at this staircase that gingerly lifts or drops boats through eight locks almost 80 feet.

Tour 2

A long but pleasant walk from the parliament buildings along Metcalfe Street will take you to the **Canadian Museum of**

Nature, 240 Metcalfe. Built in 1912, and currently undergoing extensive renovations, this elegant castle-like building is the Canadian showcase of our country's natural history. Everything from spiders and dinosaur bones to wolves and glittering gems, thousands of specimens from the Museum's huge collection are presented in six permanent exhibit halls. Continue your walk across Elgin Street to the Canal and follow the parkland trail back to the National Arts Centre.

Tour 3

On another day you must take in the Museum of Agriculture at the **Central Experimental Farm**. It is a wonderful place to visit, especially for children. The research branch of the Department of Agriculture operates the farm which is open daily to the public. There is an admission fee to the museum proper and animal barns, the rest is free. There are horse and wagon tours of the grounds which contain animal barns, greenhouses, beautiful floral gardens and an arboretum. Call 613-991-3044 for more info. The farm can be easily reached by car, bus or boat. If you are boating tie up at Hartwell's Locks, adjacent

Bytown Museum

to the farm. It is also walking distance from nearby, **Dows Lake Pavilion** which has a variety of restaurant adventures as well as bike, roller blade, canoe, and pedalboat rentals

Tour 4

Another walking tour accessible from tie up space at the Flight Locks or parking in the ByWard Market is along Sussex Drive. A detour into Majors Hill Park will bring you to the statue of Colonel By, he remains today looking out over the flight locks, his most impressive feat. It may also bring you to whatever festival happens to be going on in this park.

Continue your tour across St. Patrick Street to the **National Gallery of Canada**, 380 Sussex Drive. Built on Nepean Point in 1988, this palatial structure designed by Moshe Safdie is as much a work of art as the paintings and sculptures inside. The gallery was designed to achieve an atmosphere of openness and tranquility, where natural light pervades each exhibition area. Visitors will enjoy viewing over 40,000 works of art in this wonderful atmosphere. It is open daily, admission is free to the permanent collection, there are fees for special exhibits. Call 1-800-319-ARTS for details. A quick hike up hill to Nepean Point and the Astrolabe behind the gallery might be in order.

Across the street is the magnificent **Notre Dame Basilica**. It is quite a sight to behold inside and out.

World's Biggest Piggy Bank at the Royal Canadian Mint

Continuing up Sussex Drive discover the **Royal Canadian Mint**, at 320 Sussex. There is an admission fee yet it's sure to be an *enriching* experience. For information call 1-800-276-7714.

Further along Sussex Drive you will find yourself at **Rideau Falls** Park and the **Canada and the World Pavilion** located across the road from the Old Ottawa City Hall. Here you can view the beautiful meeting of the Ottawa and Rideau Rivers. The pavilion features internationally recognized Canadian achievements.

Past Rideau Falls you will encounter a couple of formidable embassies and the **Prime Minister's Residence** at 24 Sussex. Beyond, on the opposite side of the street, you will find yourself at **Rideau Hall,** the residence of the Governor General of Canada. Here you may tour the gardens and stately house for free, learn some history at the Visitor's Centre, have a snack at the snack bar and possibly take in an outdoor concert. This magnificent house was built by John McKay who originally came to the area to help build the canal. For information on the many events taking place here, including the hourly 'relief of sentries' from 9am-5pm, call 1-800-465-6890.

More

A side trip on your way from Ottawa to Gatineau (formerly Hull) and the Canadian Museum of Civilization is **Turtle Island**. Turtle Island offers a unique urban tourism experience in a vibrant Aboriginal Village. It is located on Victoria Island which has been a traditional gathering place for First Nations people for thousands of years. Tour packages are available and Dance presentations take place daily at

1pm and 3pm call 1-877-811-3233 for information or learn more about Turtle Island on www.aboriginalexperiences.com

Another suggested walking or bicycle tour is to **Laurier House National Historic Site**, at 355 Laurier Avenue, Laurier House commemorates two of Canada's most notable Prime Ministers, Sir Wilfrid Laurier and the Rt. Hon. William Lyon Mackenzie King. In 2004 Laurier House introduced an exciting new attraction, "Theatre on the Veranda" a theatrical experience celebrating the lives of these Prime Ministers. This new venue includes a guided tour of the house, tea, desserts and a choice of one of three short plays in a beautiful setting. Phone: 613-992-8142 www.pc.gc.ca/laurierhouse

You may be interested in a regular evening walking tour called '**The Haunted Walk of Ottawa**'. From May 1 to October 31 Ottawa's ghost stories are shared by lantern light. Call 613-232-0344 for details. www.hauntedwalk.com

If walking isn't your preferred mode of transportation perhaps you'd like to see the area by bike. There are more than 150 kms of bike paths and trails in this region and the Trans Canada Trail runs right through Ottawa and over to the Quebec side of the Ottawa River across the Alexandra Bridge. You can rent a bicycle from **Cyco's Bike Rentals** at 5 Hawthorne Avenue by the Pretoria Bridge 613-567-8180.

If your legs are tired **OC Transpo,** Ottawa's public transportation service, will get you anywhere you want to go. For fare and schedule information call 613-741-4390. You can catch the number 3 bus at Hartwells Lock or Dows Lake and it will take you straight downtown to all the big attractions. There are many modes of transport available to those wishing to tour Ottawa. Try Capital Double Decker And Trolley Tours 1-800-823-6147.

A little bit further away you can find the **National Museum of Science and Technology** (613-991-3044) at 1867 St. Laurent Blvd. a rainy day treat for kids and grown-ups alike. As well as the **National Aviation Museum** (1-800-463-2038) for the airplane buff at the junction of the Rockcliffe and Aviation Parkways. Arrangements to see them can be easily made, shuttle bus information can be found at Capital Info Centre.

Don't forget the fairs and festivals that keep tourists coming back to Ottawa, year after year. The **Canadian Tulip Festival** takes place in May. Millions of tulips annually bloom in North America's Tulip Capital, creating an exotic mosaic of colour and beauty along a 15 km Tulip route. Festivities include five official sites, and 15 attractions, visit www.tulipfestival.ca for details. The **Franco-**

Tulip Festival Flotilla,
photo courtesy of Canadian Tulip Festival

Ontarien Festival is usually held during the third week in June and features many cultural and recreational activities based on the province's French speaking culture. The **Governor General's Garden Party** takes place at the end of June, a tradition that dates back to the 1860s.

photo credit: Bill Pratt, Rideau Canal, Parks Canada

Winter on the Canal,
World's Largest Skating Rink

130

One of the highlights of winter in Ottawa is **Winterlude**. This is a winter carnival, spanning three weekends in February, featuring snow and ice sculpting, skating, skiing, entertainment and all sorts of winter fun.

Celebrating Canada at Parliament Hill
Reed, Gabby, Rowan & Alexa

photo credit: Penny Thompson

Of course there is no other place to truly celebrate **Canada Day** but in the Nation's Capital. On July 1st, there will be birthday celebrations all over the city and the biggest fireworks display of all over Parliament Hill.

Bluesfest takes place in mid-July, this outstanding music festival is soon followed by the **Ottawa International Jazz Festival**, 10 days of world class jazz, held mid to late July and attracts jazz fans and musicians from far and wide.

Ottawans celebrate **Colonel By Day** on the August Civic Holiday. The Bytown Museum is host to an array of great activities for the whole family. The **Central Canadian Exhibition** which is usually held in mid-August features agricultural exhibits, horse shows, concerts and a midway. Just to name a few, visit www.capcan.ca for more event listings.

View of Ottawa River and Museum of Civilization in Hull/Gatineau from look out at flight locks near the Bytown Museum

Ottawa Locks: 1-8

When Colonel By arrived at Wrightstown, now Gatineau, in 1826 he decided to base his canal building operation in Sleigh Bay. This long inlet was well protected and seemed an ideal place to start building the flight of locks required to surmount the high limestone ridge at the Ottawa River. It had been decided to bypass the lower section of the Rideau River as it was far too shallow and full of rapids to navigate. The plateau above Sleigh Bay was surveyed at a height of 80 feet. Samuel Clowes, the original surveyor, had proposed a route from the Ottawa River which would join the Rideau River at Three Island Rapids. This required an enormous amount of blasting and By sought an easier route. John McTaggert was sent to survey the land between Sleigh Bay and Hogs Back Rapids to determine a better route for a canal. Once completed it turned out to be a much shorter and less difficult route than Clowes had proposed. Inaccurate surveying would become problematic throughout the building of the Rideau.

Originally, By had planned to build two sets of flight locks, each consisting of four locks with a basin dividing each flight. The locks were to be 20 feet by 108 feet to accommodate gunboats, but when the Kempt Committee decided that lock chambers should be able to accommodate steamships, the chambers had to be enlarged to 33 feet by 134 feet. This decision immediately ruled out the possibility of a basin. There was no longer room for one. Excavation began in 1827

Flight locks, canal entrance, Chart 1512-1   photo credit: Canadian Hydrographic Service

and was no easy task. Because of springs in the bedrock, the work-site was very soggy in spite of drainage channels and continuous pumping. The first three locks, which had been built to earlier specifications, had to be disman-tled and rebuilt. The locks, con-structed from limestone cut from the surrounding cliffs, span the highest and longest distance on the Rideau. They were completed in 1831. Sleigh Bay is now called Entrance Bay. The Commissariat, built in 1827, is located beside the locks and was the main store house for the British Military. Today, the exterior has been restored and the Commissariat now houses the **Bytown Museum** and a Parks Canada exhibition of the Builders of the Canal.

The eight locks here will drop you a total of 79 feet/24 m into the Ottawa River. Lock-through procedure takes about 1 1/2 hours. There is plenty of tie-up space upstream of the flight locks and 150 feet of tie-up space downstream. The wash-rooms at the lockstation close at night. Gas is avail-able down-stream about four miles from the lock at the **Rockcliffe Boathouse.**

Gatineau

This now bustling city was once called Wrightstown. Philemon Wright first arrived near the falls with a group of like-minded settlers around 1796 to establish a farming community. Within a few years they had achieved enviable crops of wheat and potatoes with no readily accessible market. The overland trek to Montreal was costly and treacherous. It was not long afterward that Wright recognized the profits available from the lumber business. Transport was no problem as the lumber could easily be rafted down the Ottawa River to Montreal. The lumbering business drew many settlers to the area and by 1826, the village boasted several sawmills, grist mills, a tannery, two distilleries, a blacksmith's shop and a tavern.

In 1851, Ezra Eddy settled in Wrightstown and succeeded in starting a business which has carried his name to this day. What started as a sawmill, expanded to become a large operation which produced wooden matches and washboards and eventually became a pulp and paper plant. In 1875, Wrightstown was renamed Hull and was incorporated. The new city of Gatineau encompasses the territory of the former cities of Aylmer, Buckingham, Gatineau, Hull, and Masson-Angers. It officially came into being on January 1st, 2002.

Gatineau is closely allied with Ottawa and many of the Federal Government branches are based here. Because of the French influ-

Sailboats at rest, Ottawa River, New Edinburgh Boathouse
Photo Credit: Penny Thompson

ence, Gatineau has a very different atmosphere than Ottawa. The downtown Hull sector is renown for its night life. There are a variety of clubs, bistros, restaurants and discotheques to cater to any taste and, in Quebec, liquor is served until 3:00 a.m.

At 100 Laurier Street, is the site of the **Museum of Civilization**. The Grand Hall of the museum is the size of a football field and about five stories high. Here you'll discover 1000 years of human history. It is also home to the acclaimed Canadian Children's Museum. Admission is charged but it is well worth the visit. Another feature is the Cinema which offers both IMAX and OMNIMAX movies.

Ottawa River Cruises Tour Boat on Ottawa River, Canadian Museum of Civilization

On June 24th, French Canadians celebrate **St. Jean de Baptiste Day**. **Canada Day** celebrations on July 1st usually take place in Jacques Cartier Park. In August the exciting **International Cycling Festival** takes place at Jacques-Cartier Park. On Labour Day Weekend the **Gatineau Hot Air Balloon Festival** takes place. 150 Hot Air balloons taking off at the same time is quite a sight to see. The Festival includes fairground rides and fireworks. Information is available by calling 819-243-2331.

Gatineau Park is a beautiful tract of parkland and a wildlife sanctuary containing in excess of 80,000 acres. It is operated by the National Capital Commission. There are camping areas within the park and they operate on a first come first serve basis. The lakes in the park have both good swimming and excellent fishing.

Also in Gatineau Park is Kingsmere-Moorside, which was the summer home of William Lyon Mackenzie King, Canada's 10th Prime Minister. The house is now a museum and is open to the public, as are the tea room and dining room. The area is a maze of hiking trails which become cross-country ski trails in the winter. Information and reservations: (819) 827-2020.

The **Casino du Lac Leamy** located at 1 Boul. du Casino, is open from 9:00a.m. to 4:00a.m. to those 18 years and older and offers gaming tables, slot machines, a variety of restaurants, bars, top name entertainment, hotel accommodation and more. If you are in the gambling mood, shuttle buses from Ottawa are available. The Casino also offers free docking facilities with electricity and drinking water. In order to ensure an available docking space and your privileged access to the Casino, it is recommended that you reserve 24 hours in advance. Reservations can be made by calling (819) 772-2100 or 1 800 665-2274. If travelling by car, a magnificent tree lined drive and fabulous view of Leamy Lake will direct you to the Casino du Lac Leamy's exquisite entrance. It boasts a spectacular fountain in the middle of the lake. Apart from the gaming and restaurant facilities, light shows and concerts entertain patrons day and night. Spectacular fireworks displays occur over the lake throughout the summer.

Casino du Lac Leamy

Waterway Neighbours

photo credit:
Rideau Canal,
Parks Canada
Archive

1000 Islands * St. Lawrence * Quebec's Canals
Lake Ontario * Trent-Severn Waterway *
New York State Canals

Gananoque

Gananoque, Kingston's neighbour to the east, is well worth a visit. On the north bank of the St. Lawrence River, in the heart of the 1000 Islands, lies this beautiful town. Historic buildings, museums, theatres, festivals, beautiful inns, gourmet dining, awesome boating, cruises and more await your discovery.

The fishing is terrific too - marinas, lodges, tourist resorts and campgrounds cater to boaters and anglers alike. Its official welcome sign says it all "Gateway to the 1000 Islands". Unique shops and exquisite restaurants, not to mention sensational B&Bs are downtown. The 1000 Islands Charity Casino for the gambler. And the 1000 Islands Playhouse, Eastern Ontario's most popular summer theatre, sits right on the waterfront. Call 613-382-7020 or visit www.thousandislandsplayhouse.com for box office info.

Historic Half Moon Bay has welcomed visitors to non-denominational worship services for over 50 years. Small boats and dinghies anchor in the beautiful natural rock bay to sing hymns and listen to guest speakers.

The **Festival of the Islands** takes place every August and is one of Eastern Ontario's largest celebrations. It is 10 days of nonstop fun, concerts, historical reenactments, exhibitions, craft fairs, fireworks, antique boat show, famous Island Shore Breakfasts, scuba treasure hunts, midway, children's theatre and more. For details visit www.festivaloftheislands.com

Gananoque is the best place to board a tour boat and take in all the beauty and wonder of the 1000 Islands. Many different cruise boats to choose from offer dinner cruise and theatre packages. Here you'll find great diving opportunities too. Shallow shipwrecks have become time capsules to explore.

Watching the boats in the harbour at Gananoque Municipal Marina

Gananoque Municipal Marina
In the ♥ of the 1000 Islands

200 Seasonal Slips ~ 150 Transient Slips
Open 7 days a week ~ May 15 - mid October
Reservations accepted
Call 613-382-4088
We monitor V.H.F. Channel 68

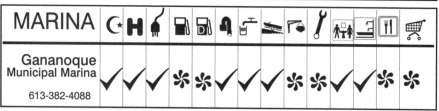

MARINA	☪	H													
Gananoque Municipal Marina 613-382-4088	✓	✓	✓	✽	✽	✓	✓	✓	✽	✽	✓	✓	✽	✽

Gananoque Visitor Welcome Centre

Boaters can reach Gananoque either through popular 10 mile Bateau Channel between the north shore of the St. Lawrence or through Admiralty Islands in the main channel.

Call 1-800-561-1595 for info about Gananoque or visit gananoque.com or 1000islands-gananoque.com

The 1000 Islands is a unique vacation destination that spans two nations. Experience friendly atmosphere on both sides of the border, and a blending of cultures in this magical region. For over 100 years summer visitors have been flocking to the 1000 Islands rich in history and natural beauty.

The St. Lawrence Seaway itself is a main shipping route and can only accommodate vessels of more than 20 ft. and 1000 kg in weight. The seaway locks cannot allow smaller vessels for safety reasons. Towns on both sides of the Seaway offer many delights and sights to see. On the Canadian side Cornwall, Morrisburg, Iroquois, Prescott, Brockville, Rockport, Ivy Lea, Gananoque and Kingston all offer nearby full service marinas, historical interest, shops, accommodation and dining. For information on the St. Lawrence contact The St. Lawrence Seaway Authority at 202 Pitt St. Cornwall, Ontario K6J 3P7 or call 613-932-5170 or email: marketing @seaway.ca or visit www.seaway.ca

The **St. Lawrence Islands National Park** is part of the 1000 (1,865 in fact) islands scattered across the St. Lawrence River where it meets Lake Ontario. It can be found between Kingston and Brockville. Sixteen islands, parts of six other islands, numerous rock shoals and a mainland base at Mallory Landing make up Canada's smallest national park. Docking, trails, shelters and camping facilities can be found on most islands. Contact St. Lawrence Islands National Park, 2 County Road 5, R.R. 3 Mallorytown, Ontario K0E 1R0 or call 613-923-5261 for more information.

For drivers, the **1000 Islands Parkway** is a self directed touring route beginning in Gananoque and carrying on east along the river to the hidden treasures awaiting you in the communities of Ivy Lea, Rockport, Hill Island and Lansdowne.

*Sailing into Gananoque
Municipal Marina*

Quebec's Canals

Lachine Canal in the heart of Montreal

The Lachine Canal runs through the heart of Montreal, with trails for walking, jogging or cycling alongside. It was instrumental in the expansion of navigation on the St. Lawrence. The Carillon Canal, with its awe-inspiring 20 metre high lock, is one of the earliest canals on the Ottawa River, and was built for military puposes linking Montreal, Ottawa and Kingston. The Chambly Canal is located on the Richelieu River 51 kms upriver of St.-Ours. Saint -Ours Canal is located 23 kms from Sorel on the Richelieu and bypasses the final obstacle to navigation between the St. Lawrence and Lake Champlain. St. Anne-de-Bellevue Canal allows vessels to navigate between Lake Saint-Louis and Lac des Deux Montagne at the mouth of the Ottawa River.

All presenting the fascinating story of this country's demographic and economic development, the canals at Lachine, Carillon, Chambly, Saint-Ours and Sainte-Anne-de-Bellevue offer boaters a network of wonderful inland waterways. The Quebec Canal's are operated by Parks Canada call (450) 447-4888 or 1-800-463-6769 or write 1899 Perigny Blvd., Chambly, Quebec, J3L 4C3 for more information. Visit their web-site: www.parcscanada.risq.qc.ca/canaux

20 metre high Lock at Carillon Canal on the Ottawa River

The Ports of Lake Ontario offer excellent marine services and beautiful cities to visit. West of Kingston are Belleville, Trenton and Cobourg.

Belleville: Billed as "the choice location", Belleville offers big city amenities along with small town friendliness, and a pleasing mixture of the historic and modern. Located on the Bay of Quinte this is home to an excellent yacht harbour which is a picturesque stopping point for Great Lakes sailors, and a favourite launch for sportfishing enthusiasts after walleye, pike and bass. In the winter Belleville becomes a major ice fishing centre. Each July thousands of visitors enjoy the **Waterfront Festival & Folklorama**, while year round beautiful music chimes from the City Hall clock tower overlooking the civic square and farmers market.

Visitors will also find the city convenient to the Bay of Quinte region with its beaches, museums, bird migrations, racing facilities, factory outlets and First Nations attractions. Touring is a fascinating adventure along the Loyalist Parkway, the Cheese Route and the Apple Route all nearby. Belleville is conveniently located on Hwy 401, and is definitely worth a visit. Belleville offers excellent hotels, motels, campgrounds, marinas, picnic areas and fine restaurants. Docking facilities are located adjacent to the downtown core giving boaters access to every shopping need. Call 1-888-852-9992 for more.

Trenton: Trenton is situated on the Murray Canal which connects the Bay of Quinte to Lake Ontario. It also is home to the first locks of the Trent-Severn Waterway. The Fraser Park Marina welcomes boaters and is a Canada Customs check point. It is steps from downtown and all amenities are available here. Call the Qunite West Chamber for more information on Trenton at 1-800-930-3255 or visit the Chamber of Commerce website at www.quintewestchamber.on.ca.

Fraser Park Marina, Trenton

Cobourg: When approaching the Murray Canal and Trenton from the west, boaters can dock at several welcoming ports that will offer excellent overnight docking accommodations for provisions and fuel or safety during rough weather. Cobourg is situated on a sandy stretch of Lake Ontario shoreline. A vibrant and charming community, this town has a rich and intriguing history enthusiastically expressed in the splendid heritage buildings around town. Boaters can enjoy a leisurely walk to fine stores and restaurants in the downtown area, just 5 minutes from the marina or for added convenience bicycles are available free of charge at the marina office. Cobourg displays friendly small town charm, offering visitors a multitude of things to do and see, including summer concerts in Victoria Park and exceptional shows in magnificent Victoria Hall.

The visitor information centre is located in Dressler House, 212 King Street West birthplace of 1930's Oscar winning actress Marie Dressler. Cobourg is a hub of activities during the summer season. Contact the Chamber of Commerce at 1-888-COBOURG for details and a calendar of events.

Cobourg Harbour

Trent-Severn Waterway

The Trent-Severn Waterway is a 240-mile/386 km heritage canal system operated by Parks Canada that meanders across central Ontario linking Lake Ontario and Georgian Bay. For boaters and land-based visitors alike, this picturesque inland waterway offers a host of unique vacation and exploration opportunities.

The waterway extends from Trenton in the south to Port Severn in the north. It is made up of four principal river systems, the Trent, Otonabee, Talbot and Severn-as well as Rice Lake, the Kawartha Lakes chain, Lake Simcoe and Lake Couchiching. The Trent-Severn route is steeped in history, culture, attractions and ever-changing scenery from gently rolling farmland to rugged Canadian Shield country. While envisaged as a prime commercial transportation and shipping route back in the 1830s construction of the extensive lock network to bring the dream to reality was sporadic. It wasn't until 1920 that full navigation of the waterway was possible. Today the Trent-Severn like the Rideau Canal has evolved into a recreational boating paradise.

Inviting communities dot the waterway's path where boaters can conveniently replenish supplies, explore, shop, dine and savour a variety of music and drama festivals, art shows and interesting museums that tell the Trent-Severn's varied history. Ports of call include Trenton, Campbellford, Hastings, Peterborough, Lakefield, Bridgenorth, Buckhorn, Bobcaygeon, Fenelon Falls, Lindsay, Barrie and Orillia. All of these small cities, towns and quaint villages have the welcome mat out each boating season for visitors cruising the waterway or arriving by land wanting to rent a boat to explore different parts of the waterway or take in some excellent fishing opportunities for which many sections of the route is famous.

Over the past decade many municipalities have invested in their waterfronts installing and upgrading marinas, beaches, camping and picnic areas to ensure boaters and other waterway guests can really enjoy all the Trent-Severn has to offer.

Hastings on the Trent is the gateway to Rice Lake, the second largest lake on the Trent system. Since 1615, when Samuel Champlain is said to have navigated this historical site, to 1820 when the town was named Crook's Rapids, and onward to today, people discover abundant wildlife along the 1500 feet of greenbelt marina and picnic area. Watch for Great Blue Herons, muskrats and beavers. Or enjoy a swim at the public beach. Relax on the 70 foot' waterfront deck at the new municipal marina and waterfront walkway – a great place to dock your boat. From here, you can stroll to the first dam ever built on the Trent in 1844 and marvel at the highest velocity of Trent water shooting through the dam chutes as anglers compete for trophy fish from the bridge. After this kick up your feet and have some lunch fare while patio dining at the water's edge or sample gourmet coffee at the new chic lock-side café.If you are in need of more to do there is 5-pin bowling, century homes to enjoy, pontoon boat and personal watercraft rentals, or just stock up on supplies at the LCBO and grocers' and even catch up on your banking. Chat with our veterans at the Legion and relax a while.

With 60 kilometres of lock-free open water, Hastings is a great choice to stay overnight - or dock your vessel for the season! And at the end of it all, watch spectacular sunsets from the deck of your yacht as you prepare for yet another day at Hastings, the Hub of the Trent.

Rice Lake's open water leads to the Otonabee River before reaching Peterborough, a city of some 75,000 people and Peterborough Marina positioned in the heart of the city surrounded by Del Crary Park. This marine park is home to the famous summer Festival of Lights--offer-

ing outstanding and absolutely free open-air musical concerts running mid-June through the end of August every Wednesday and Saturday night. Overnight docking reservations are encouraged! Peterborough is also home to the Canadian Canoe Museum, which offers visitors a glimpse into the country's canoeing heritage and what is touted as the largest and most varied collection of canoes in the world. One of the highlights of any Trent-Severn cruise is experiencing the "lift of your life" at the Peterborough Lift Lock just beyond Peterborough Marina. This engineering marvel turned 100 years old in 2004. It's a double tub hydraulic lift lock with a vertical lift of 65 feet---the highest of its kind in the world!

Kawartha Lakes Country

Further up river, the historic village of **Lakefield** straddles both sides of the Otonabee River. And as the Chamber of Commerce motto says, this is the true Gateway to the Kawarthas---the outstanding chain of lakes that include Katchewanooka, Stony, Lovesick, Buckhorn and Pigeon. This is the beginning of real rugged cottage country offering visitors a host of cruising and vacationing options from four star resorts to more humble fishing lodges. While a complete Trent-Severn cruise should take two weeks it would be easy to spend that much time just exploring the entire Kawartha Lakes Country region has to offer.

Exploring all Lakefield has to offer will take a day alone. While the village's excellent marina is closed temporarily for upgrades, there's ample tie up space along the canal wall just upstream from the lock station. A quaint downtown along Queen Street is always bustling with visitors trying out the new bistros or picking up a special picnic lunch or gourmet dinner to go offered at *In A Nuttshell*. Further along others languish on the veranda of a coffee house or are coming and going from the new 26-room Victorian style *Village Inn* that recently

opened its doors to guests along with restaurant and pub. In the early 1800s Lakefield was the home of pioneer families like Moodie, Strickland and Traill. Sisters Susanna Moodie and Catherine Parr Traill now famous writings give today's readers a spectacular look at what 'Roughing It in The Bush' was really like! Stop by *HappenStance Books & Yarns* and find out why Lakefield is dubbed the cradle of Canadian literature. One of Lakefield's most historic sites is the tiny stone Christ Church, built in 1853. Today it's a museum showcasing a number of historical artifacts including Catherine Parr Traill's writing desk. At the rear of the church property is Lakefield's pioneer cemetery facing the waterfront.

Lakefield, now incorporated in the amalgamated townships of Smith-Ennismore-Lakefield, which covers most of Kawartha Lake country shoreline, has always worked diligently to protect and enhance its community waterfront. The village offers its residents and visitors the opportunity to wander along more than 5 kilometres of groomed trails that flank both riverbanks and link with parks, a huge marsh conservation area, campground and swimming beach.

Even the more than century old waterfront waiting station, where tourists used to take steam boats inland to the different lakes before good roads opened this region, has been preserved. For close to a century Lakefield was also known for its cedar strip canoe and boat building industry. The old *Brown Canoe Company* building still stands off Queen Street now transformed into an upscale giftware, furniture and clothing store which also sports a great fly fishing supply centre.

If you didn't bring your own boat to the Kawartha Lakes it doesn't matter. There are lots of places to rent smaller runabouts for waterway touring or day fishing trips. Houseboating is also a very popular vacation pastime on these sheltered lakes. These small fully equipped floating lodges let visitors explore at a leisurely pace and are one of the best ways to experience all the scenery and fun events that abound in the Kawarthas.

For day trippers and weekend visitors there are several large cruise boats that ply the waters offering close up views of historical sites and excellent supporting commentary. These cruise boat operators also offer special evening dinner/dancing cruises for more lake fun under the stars. Speaking of fun, Kawartha Lakes communities stage many annual festivals each year. There's everything from art, jazz, wine and cheese to buskers on the loose. The area is rich in native culture too with art galleries showcasing native art and unique heritage sites like the Petroglyphs where ancient rock paintings can be viewed.

This snapshot about the Trent-Severn and its many and equally exciting regions will hopefully whet your appetite to learn more about this great waterway and the vacation adventures that await traditional cruising boaters and land lubbers alike!

For more information about the Trent-Severn contact Friends of the Trent-Severn Waterway, P.O. Box 572, Peterborough, Ontario, K9J 6Z6, 705-742-2251 or www.ftsw.com or call FTSW 1-800-663-2628.

Contact the Kawartha Lakes Chamber of Commerce (Eastern Region) in Lakefield. See ad in this section for numbers and web site. This Chamber of Commerce is also part of a tourism marketing partnership involving other Kawartha region Chambers of Commerce serving lake country and will be pleased to steer your more detailed requests in the right direction.

To help plan your trip you may wish to purchase a copy of the *Trent-Severn Waterway Boating and Road Guide* call 1-800-324-6052 or visit www.ontariotravelguides.com to find out where it is available.

New York State Canals

The New York State Canal System is a navigable, 524-mile inland waterway comprised of four Canals: the **Erie**, **Champlain**, **Cayuga-Seneca** and **Oswego** Canals. On the eastern end of the state, the Champlain canal runs 63 miles from Troy, to Whitehall on the southern end of Lake Champlain. The Oswego canal at 24 miles long, connects the Erie near Syracuse with Lake Ontario. The Cayuga & Seneca canal is 27 miles long and connects the Erie, west of Syracuse with Cayuga and Seneca Lakes. The Erie Canal today is 363 miles long, has 57 locks and the total rise from the Hudson River to Lake Erie is 568 feet.

This network of inland waterways is a popular tourism destination each year for thousands of pleasure boaters and offers visitors many unique attractions, historic sites, museums, parks, picnic areas, restaurants, inns and dozens of community festivals taking place in charming port towns and bustling cities. Across the Canal region, visitors are invited to step back in time and relive the early Canal days. Along this historic corridor, visitors of all ages can enjoy more than 2,500 recreational facilities and attractions. There are 200 marinas and launch sites located along New York State's canals.

This Canal System connects with hundreds of miles of lakes and rivers across New York State, and links the Great Lakes with the Hudson River and with Canada's waterways -including the Rideau Canal.

For more information on New York State Canals call toll free: 1-800-4CANAL4.

For further information about Boating Regulations, Boat Launches, Camping and Historic Sites write to NYS Office of Parks, Recreation and Historic Preservation Agency Building 1, Empire State Plaza Albany, NY 12238. Call for information. 518-474-0456 http://nysparks.state.ny.us/info/

Useful websites include:
www.canals.state.ny.us/
www.eriecanal.org
www.nycanal.com
www.bargecanals.com
www.canals.state.ny.us

Ottawa River

Waterway

Arnprior to Temiskaming Shores

Ottawa River Waterway

*S*tretching from Arnprior, just west of Ottawa, nearly 500 kilometers north to the City of Temiskaming Shores, the Ottawa River Waterway, formerly the Temiskawa Waterway, is tailor-made for smaller, trailerable boats.

Unlike standard locks, the Ottawa River Waterway, bypasses rapids and dams using tow vehicles hooked to marine hydraulic trailers capable of handling power boats up to 30 feet in length and 12,000 pounds of displacement for one to two-kilometer distance. Pontoon boats as long as 28 feet can be moved on special bunk trailers. Unfortunately, due to trailer design and clearance, houseboats and sailboats not equipped with retractable keels and quick-stepping masts cannot be accommodated.

Bypass sites for each of the five lifts (located on both sides of the provincial border at Temiscaming, Mattawa, Rapides-des-Joachims, Desjardinville, Chapeau, Bryson and Portage-du-Fort) feature modern docks and concrete ramps. Some offer additional amenities to make overnight stays at the docks more convenient. You must however, book 24 hours in advance to reserve your lift. The entire process, from haul-outs to re-launch, usually takes 20 to 30 minutes.

Following water routes used by native people and Canada's earliest explorers, the Ottawa River Waterway delivers an unusual mix of scenic wilderness cruising and onshore amenities found at easily accessible full-service marinas and the towns and cities along the Ottawa River bordering Ontario and Quebec.

Navigation is straightforward and major obstacles are well-marked and charted. With the recent completion of charting Lake Temiskaming, official nautical charts now cover the entire Ottawa River Waterway. Canadian Hydrographic Services Charts 1551-1556 can be obtained at most local marinas or see page 7 in this guide for chart dealers. In addition, the website www.ottawariverwaterway.com

will provide detailed navigational information on the Waterway and insight on its communities, services and attractions. Call toll-free 1-866-224-5244 for more information.

Whether you plan on a weekend getaway or two-week vacation, you'll discover a rich variety of events, attractions, restaurants and shopping along the Ottawa River Waterway. There's no shortage of overnight accommodation either. You can spend a restful night on the water, anchored in a sheltered cove, or camp onshore. Less adventurous boaters can enjoy a comfortable night's sleep in one of the many hotels, motels or lodges enroute, or docked at well equipped community marinas.

The Ottawa River Waterway can be accessed from many locations between the City of Temiskaming Shores and Notre-Dame-du-Nord in the north and Arnprior in the south. The waterway is also a gateway to the regions several prime backwater lakes, rivers and thriving communities.

The deep waters of Lake Temiskaming mark the northern boundary of the Ottawa River Waterway. Haileybury, now part of the newly amalgamated City of Temiskaming Shores including Haileybury, New Liskeard and Dymond, is located on the west shore, and is a prime example of northeastern Ontario hospitality and boater friendly facilities earmarked by a newly developed waterfront, full-service marina, sandy beach and great fishing for bass, pike and walleye. Haileybury is also home to a world-famous mining school (attended by many executives worldwide) and a heritage museum. Devil's Rock, named after an Indian princess who leaped to her death after being denied marriage to the brave she chose, offers a spectacular view of the lake. It is also widely considered to be the setting for the *House on the Cliff,* one of the books in the famous Hardy Boys series.

Five miles north is New Liskeard, which also boasts a full service marina, restaurants shopping, museums and other attractions. While in Temiskaming Shores, also participate in Temiskaming Treasure Tours, an interesting guided tour of the area including a visit to Cobalt, Canada's Silver Mining Capital, recent-

ly named as 'Ontario's Most Historical Town'.

Every weekend during the summer months a host of interesting events are held which may peak the interest of most every boater. Starting from the northern most extremity of the waterway at Notre-Dame du Nord, the *Rodeo Camion* is held every July which attracts 35,000 annually to a truck pull, show and shine celebration. While in Notre-Dame du Nord, visit the *Fossil Museum* which tracks the evolution of the planet over the past billions of years. Or take a tour of the Riviere de Quinze power generation plant. Twenty-five miles south on the Quebec side, Ville Marie hosts the annual *Foire Gourmande "Food Fair"* which features a wide variety of regional foods. While at Ville Marie's full service marina, take a walk to *La Grotto*, a Catholic religious tribute to the 12 Stations of the Cross overlooking the town, visit their *St-Augustine Chenier Gallery.* Take a short boat ride or a longer hike and tour Parks Canada's *Fort Temiskaminque* which interactively high-lights the Hudson Bay & NorthWest fur trading era.

There are many events and sites along the Ottawa River Waterway,

from Opemika Falls and Opemika Point Steam Boat Shop, to Mattawa and their *Voyageur Days*, and to Deep River, Petawawa, Pembroke and Arnprior that hosts various Canada Day events and Waterfront festivals. The calendar of events can be downloaded from the website.

Pembroke is one the first stops for boaters with their compasses pointed North. Located in the heart of the Ottawa Valley, the city features a recently revamped waterfront (with an annual August festival), marina services, an extensive choice of accommodations and, like much of northeastern Ontario, access to some of the most productive angling waters. Pembroke is also known for excellent bird watching. Nearby *Driftwood Provincial Park* offers family camping, boating facilities and superlative sandy beaches.

A short distance upriver, captains and crews can dock and visit Petawawa's *Canadian Airborne Forces Museum*, which showcases an array of indoor exhibits illustrating the country's 45 year history of military parachuting, and outdoor displays of vehicles and aircraft.

Deep River, a two-hour drive from Ottawa caters to sail and power boaters. There's a yacht club and a select number of marinas offering limited transient slips on a first-come, first served basis. Deep River also lays claim to being one of the smallest communities in the country to have its own symphony orchestra and Canada's sole heritage clock museum.

The Ottawa River is rich in wilderness and diverse in culture, your boating experience will truly be a memorable one.

Information Sources:

Ottawa River Waterway
1 Pembroke St. East, P.O. Box 277, Pembroke, Ontario K8A 6X3
Phone: 613-735-5416 Toll Free: 1-866-224-5244
www.ottawariverwaterway.com or E-mail: info@ottawariverwaterway.com

Ottawa Valley Tourist Information 1-800-757-6580 (613) 732-4364
www.ottawavalley.org

MRC Pontiac 1-800-665-5217 www.mrcpontiac.qc.ca

City of Pembroke (613) 735-6821 www.pembroke.ca

City of Temiskaming Shores Tourism Information (705) 647-5709
www.temiskamingshores.ca

Abitibi-Temiscamingue Tourist Information 1-800-808-0706 www.48nord.qc.ca

Ville Marie Tourist Information 1-866-538-3647

Mattawa Tourist Information 1-800-267-4222 www.voyageurdays.com

Temiscaming Tourist Information 1-866-538-3647 www.temiscaming.net

Tourism Outaouais 1-800-265-7822 www.tourisme-outaouais.ca

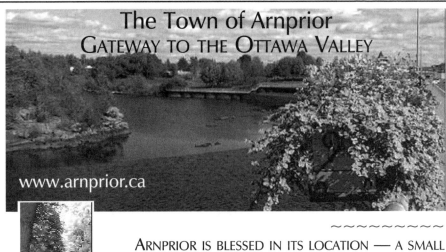

Arnprior: The Town of Two Beautiful Rivers

Arnprior is located at the junction of the Ottawa and Madawaska Rivers. This Port of Call is situated on the doorstep of the nation's capital, at the west end of Highway 417 and Lanark County Road 29, and is the southern gateway to the beautiful Ottawa Valley and Ottawa River Waterway.

If arriving by boat, dock at the **Municipal Marina**, which is open from the long weekend in May until the second last weekend in October. Berths may be booked on a seasonal, monthly or daily basis. There are 84 docks as well as 12 transient slips, which may be booked weekly or daily. Dock hands are on site to help boaters All piers are secured by locked doors with only boaters and staff having access. The Marina is governed by the Town of Arnprior, with suggestions coming through a Marina Subcommittee made up of seasonal boaters. Docking and seasonal rates are competitive. Transient slips rent for just $16 per

day. Arnprior's convenient location offers boaters a key starting point for an Ottawa River Waterway cruising vacation. Boaters can launch their craft at the launch ramp ($5.00 in & $5.00 out), shop for provisions, gas up at the service dock and be on your way in no time.

The Marina is connected to a renowned Millennium Trails System, which allows residents and visitors alike a picturesque walk through this beautiful community. **The Gillies Trail** winds along the west side of the Madawaska River from the weir in the centre of town, past the town's Marina and on into Robert Simpson Park. From there, you can visit the Gillies Grove through the Galilee Mission entrance.

The Heritage Trail wanders through the historic downtown residential and commercial districts, which feature late-19th and early 20th-century homes and buildings, including Arnprior's signature structure the Gillies Building. This building houses the Arnprior & District Museum, which is open from mid-June to mid-Sept.

Museum Admission:
Adults $2.50 Students & Seniors $1.50 Family $8.00 Children under 8 free
Phone 613•623•4902 for more information

The McLachlin Trail starts on the west side of the Madawaska River and stretches from the weir to Bell Park on the Ottawa River. Bell Park was donated to the youth of Arnprior by the grandchildren of James and Kathleen Bell in memory of happy summers spent with their grandparents in this area. As you follow the trail towards the point, you will pass the Yacht Club and the Fish and Game Club. Bell Park, located at the conjunction of the Madawaska and Ottawa Rivers, has a beautiful view of the Quebec shoreline and the widened section of the Ottawa River known as Chats Lake (Lac des Chats).

Developed at the same time as the Millennium Trails was the Macnamara Trail, which starts just a stone's throw from the McLean Avenue beach across from the Arnprior Amateur Ball Association diamonds. This trail continues through the Nopiming Game Preserve, a game sanctuary since 1920. Nopiming is an Indian term meaning "in the woods." Access to the preserve is courtesy of Honeywell Nylon Canada Inc., which owns the land. The trail is maintained by the Macnamara Field Naturalists' Club. As well, the town maintains walking/biking trails along the former railway line, including a newly developed park in the heart of the town.

There are 12 neighbourhood parks in Arnprior, but by far the greatest jewel in the crown of Arnprior's park system is **Robert Simpson Park**, which is located in town at the confluence of the Ottawa and Madawaska Rivers. The Park features beachfront on the Ottawa River, a bandstand on a hill overlooking the river, a sand and water play structure, flower gardens planted by local school children and (maintained by community volunteers and Parks staff), and acres of treed parkland and open space.

THE GILLIES GROVE

A few minutes walk from Robert Simpson Park is the magnificent **Gillies Grove** — nearly 45 acres of Old Growth forest. Gillies Grove is a rare remnant of the magnificent forest that once covered this region and is one of the last such tracts in the province. The Grove's unique natural environment harbours multitudes of creatures, some quite rare and elusive. The Grove is also home to a rich array of plant life.

Rideau by Paddle

photo credit: Bill Pratt, Rideau Canal, Parks Canada

'Paddling the Rideau Canal'

Canadian Recreational Canoeing Association

Paddling the Rideau Canal

A Guide to Canoeing and Kayaking *by: Don MacKay*

The Rideau Canal stretches 202 km from Kingston to Ottawa, connecting boaters and visitors with an earlier time when canal building was a means of improving trade and defending a growing nation. Today the canal offers the perfect setting for relaxation and recreation, particularly for the paddler.

The Rideau system encompasses 47 locks, 24 lockstations, historic buildings, and two large watersheds: the Rideau and the Cataraqui. The canal was built in the early 19th century under the direction of Lt. Colonel John By of the British Royal Engineers, but native people of the area had been travelling the lakes and rivers of the Rideau route for centuries. In fact, only 19 kilometers of the system is cut channel. The Rideau offers a number of natural paddling environments — lakes, rivers and wetlands – showcasing the beauty and diversity of the system. Imagine yourself gliding across the calm waters of the Rideau on a crisp, bright September morning … the following tips will bring you closer to this enjoyable Rideau Canal experience.

Some hints and suggestions on paddling the canal:

Class of Paddling. Open lake with capsize potential on the large lakes, particularly in extreme conditions such as thunderstorms and strong winds, and Class I river (so long as you avoid the dams - Class IV to Class VI).

Best Time to Paddle. The shoulder season: May, June, September and October.

Why?
• Fewer powerboats, moderate temperatures.
• Best choice of places to pitch a tent and watch an amazing sunset or invigorating sunrise.

Paddling During Peak Season. If you wish to paddle during the height of powerboat season (July and August), the trip can still be fantastic. Unlike powerboats, canoes and kayaks do not have to follow the channel. In fact, most paddlers prefer to follow the shoreline and take a less direct route from one lock to another, away from the noise and wake of powerboats, and closer to interesting sights on shore. You may even decide to portage into the canal's numerous feeder lakes and rivers.

Paddling Environment (Following the navigation route). The canal offers five different paddling environments: lakes (various sizes and depths), marshes, open rivers, narrow channels, and populated rivers.

photo credit: Bill Pratt, Rideau Canal, Parks Canada

a)***Kingston to Upper Brewers Locks*** - Starts with the Cataraqui Marsh (Class I Wetland) followed by Kingston Mills Lockstation and Colonel By Lake (a shallow, stump littered lake with a shoreline of low rocks and few trees, it expanded as a result of flooding during the construction of the Rideau). The lake leads into a narrow channel and canal with cattails, grasses and overhanging trees.

A great place to paddle and to escape the wind (with the exception of Colonel By Lake, which can become quite rough) with few interruptions. Camping at all lockstations.

b)***Upper Brewers Locks to Narrows Lock (including the Big Rideau)*** – Beautiful, clear, scenic lakes with natural shorelines featuring local flora and fauna. Short sections of canal as you enter and exit lockstations along the way. This stretch of the canal is the most popular with boaters and visitors. Great for swimming and fishing. There are many bays and islands – an ideal atmosphere for paddling.

c)***Beveridges Locks to Long Island Locks*** - Marsh, winding canal and river intermixed with smaller, shallow, flooded lakes and marshy shorelines. Preceding Detached Lockstation in Smiths Falls is the Swale (Class I Wetland), the Tay River, the Tay Marsh (Class I Wetland) and Beveridges Locks. Following Detached Lockstation, there are numerous locks that make this area an ideal choice for short day trips, with easy take-out and put-in. En route is a Federal Bird Sanctuary and Class 1 and 2 Wetlands located upstream from Merrickville.

d)***Long Island Locks to Ottawa*** - Winding canal lined with overhanging trees. The density of residential development along the shoreline increases as you approach Ottawa. An urban type of paddling – a chance to get out on the water without having to go far from the city. Largely sheltered from strong winds and waves.

MAPS - There are two excellent sources of maps:

1)The navigation charts that can be purchased at most lockstations or the main canal office in Smiths Falls.

2)Topographic maps cover a wider area (feeder lakes, rivers and streams along with highways and road access points) than the boater navigation charts.

Best Direction to Paddle. If you wish to paddle the Rideau in its entirety or to travel a large section, the best direction to paddle is from Kingston to Ottawa for two reasons.

1)The prevailing southwest winds blow in that general direction. There is nothing worse than tackling a large lake such as the Big Rideau and paddling for miles into a stiff and rough south wind.

2)As you approach Ottawa, the current becomes a factor to a small extent.

photo credit: Elisabeth McEuen, Rideau Canal, Parks Canada   *Clowes Spillway*

Safety Tips

a) For your safety, *stay away from any dams and waste weirs.* For the most part, these hazards are located near lockstations and marked with either signs or orange and white booms.

b) *Watch out for boatwash or wake, and be prepared to handle the on-coming waves* either by turning into the wave or using a low brace to stabilize the boat.

c) *Wind* - check weather forecasts before heading out, and choose your route accordingly. During a multi-day excursion, think ahead and check with lock staff as to the conditions for the next leg of your journey. Know the wind direction (not always a prevailing wind) and how this will affect your craft (head, side, or tail wind).

During periods of high water (April to mid-June), river flows/currents increase in strength and paddlers should be cautious. However, paddling current on the main channel does not exceed Class I. Other sections of the canal (dams and their run-off) can be classified as Class VI.

d) *Make sure that you carry the following equipment*: a) a lifejacket for each person, on or within easy reach; b) an extra paddle; c) a bailing can; d) a whistle or a horn for emergencies; d) a throw rope - floating type.

FEES AND FACILITIES

Camping - Camping is permitted at all lockstations along the Rideau Canal with the exception of Ottawa Locks and Combined Lockstation in Smiths Falls. (Detached Lockstation and Old Sly's Lockstation are a very short paddling distance from Combined – within eyesight). Most lockstations have drinking water, picnic tables, barbecues, and washrooms. Camping $15 per party (up to 10 people, $4.00 for each additional person).

Places to Camp or Stay other than Lockstations -

There are several options:

Camping is available on Colonel By Island on Big Rideau Lake. This government island has a beautiful two-km walking trail and an interior lake that opens onto the main lake. Lost Lake is not suitable for powerboats, but great for a nice evening or morning paddle. Deer, osprey and loons are but a few inhabitants of this island.

Murphy's Point Provincial Park, located on the Big Rideau, has several paddle-in camping areas. Rideau River Provincial Park is located near Becketts Landing northwest of Kemptville.

If you prefer other accommodations, there are a number of hotels, lodges and bed & breakfasts along the way.

Lock Passes – The Rideau Canal has developed a lock pass to meet the needs of canoeists and kayakers: the transit pass. This pass enables the paddler to travel the 202 km from one end of the system to the other (either north or south) with no time limit. It is valid for the entire season. However, once you pass through a lock you cannot go back in the opposite direction without purchasing a different type of pass.

The cost of the transit pass is $4.25 per foot, so a pass for a 16' canoe or kayak would total $68.00 (tax included). Locking is a great opportunity to rest, have some trail mix, and soak up some sun while the lock staff move you to your next level of paddling. Also, it's a great time to ask the knowledgeable staff about the best places to paddle, or how far it is to the next lake or lockstation.

If you don't wish to buy the transit pass, you may portage around the locks at no cost; or portage at smaller lockstations and buy a single lock or one day pass to eliminate long-distance portages at the large, multi-chamber lockstations.

Length of Trip (end to end) - Obviously, this depends on the weather and skill level of the paddler. In general, you should set aside 6 - 10 days to paddle the entire Rideau Canal. If you'd like to paddle the lakes and rivers throughout the Rideau and the Cataraqui watersheds, plan for an entire summer of canoe tripping.

Two Suggested Paddling Trips

Perth to Beveridges Locks (1 day)

Put-In/Take-Out: *Perth Basin or Beveridges Locks* (Port Elmsley - County Road 18) - Ample parking at either location.

Length: 12 km (7 miles)

Type of Paddling: A gentle winding river and canal with overhanging trees. Includes a section of Class I Wetland Marsh. Very relaxing and scenic with little powerboat traffic.

Hazards: None so long as you stay away from Beveridges Dam. Very protected and sheltered.

Features

a)The historic town of Perth with its many old buildings, tree-lined streets and interesting shops.

b)As you paddle down the river, you can see sections of the Pike River from which the Tay Canal was built.

c)The Tay Marsh and associated wildlife.

d)Beveridges Lockstation - this lockstation features two locks separated by a short canal. It's home to a pair of osprey nesting atop a telephone pole near the lower lock. There is an on-site exhibit and a short trail to an overlook.

Hints: The current runs from Perth to Beveridges Locks.

Upper Brewers Locks to Newboro Locks   *(2 days)*

Put-In/Take-Out: Upper Brewers Lockstation (County Road 12, off Hwy 15) and Newboro Lockstation (County Road 42, off Hwy.15). Both places offer ample parking and camping.

Length: 39 km (24 miles)

Type of Paddling: This section of the canal is almost entirely small lakes with a variety of shoreline ranging from steep cliffs to heavily forested shores.

Hazards: During extreme weather conditions, the lakes can get nasty. However, the shoreline is usually not far away.

Camping: The best place to relax the first night is Jones Falls Lockstation. Pitch a tent by the turning basin or higher up near the Horseshoe Dam. The second night, pack up or stay at Newboro Lockstation, where there are many places to pitch a tent.

Features

a)Upper Brewers Lockstation - two manually operated locks in flight.

b)A slight detour into Morton Bay from Whitefish Lake. This long, deep, narrow bay has a rocky shore with two very large rock out-croppings: "Rock Dunder" and "Dunder's Mate" on the right shore. This is an excellent spot to swim or to take a hike to the top of the rocky ledge.

c)Jones Falls Lockstation (3 locks in flight followed by a turning basin and a fourth lock). This lock also features a working blacksmith shop, a 19th-century defensible lockmaster's house with a com-manding view of the lockstation, and a 60-foot keystone arch dam which, at the time of its construction in the 1830's, was the third highest in the world and the largest in North America.

d)Davis Lock - the "wilderness lock." This lock is the most isolated of the lockstations, and is situated between two beautiful lakes. A great place to have a quiet lunch on day two.

e)Chaffey's Lock - one of the most popular on the canal. It features a stone lockmaster's house, now a local museum, and a number of excellent places to eat.

f)Newboro Lockstation - one of only three electric hydraulic locks on the Rideau. It also has one of the four blockhouses built to defend the canal from attack.

Hints: The best direction to paddle is from Upper Brewers to Newboro Lockstation so that the prevailing winds are at your back. Also, Jones Falls is a steep portage - 60 feet in vertical height if you don't buy a lock pass.

The author of this article, an experienced kayaker, is also the Blacksmith at the Jones Falls Lockstation. Drop in at Jones Falls Lockstation and visit the Blacksmith at work. (May to Mid-October)

Don MacKay, Blacksmith at work, Jones Falls Lockstation

Free Information

Available at lockstations and through Parks Canada.

"Rideau Canal - Between Kingston and Ottawa" - brief history, small overview map and list of services available at the lockstations.

"Boating Safely" (Rideau Canal and Trent-Severn Waterway) - aids to navigation information plus a chart in the back with paddling distances from lockstation to lockstation and various places in between.

"Hours of Operation and Fees" - lists the various types of passes available and the hours when locks are in operation.

The Cataraqui Region Conservation Authority has produced several suggested canoe "loop" routes that include parts of the Rideau System. Copies available from their Rideau Canal Office, or by mail at 1641 Perth Road, P.O. Box 160, Glenburnie, Ontario. K0H 1S0 Telephone: (613) 546-4228   Fax (613) 547-6474.

Useful Names, Numbers, Addresses and Information Guides

Rideau Canal Office 34A Beckwith St. S., Smiths Falls, ON K7A 2A8 Telephone 1-800-230-0016 or (613) 283-5170 E-mail: RideauCanal-info @pc.gc.ca

Web Site: http://www.pc.gc.ca/lhn-nhs/on/rideau/index_e.asp

Another source of information about the Rideau Canal is Ken Watson's Web Site: www.rideau-info.com

Exploring St. Lawrence Islands National Park: Just off the main boating channels of the St. Lawrence River, among the 1000 Islands, a fascinating world of natural sights and sounds awaits the observant paddler in back bays and small streams and along rugged natural shorelines. The best times to visit are in the spring and late summer to early fall.

For further information, write to St. Lawrence Islands National Park, R.R.3, Mallorytown, ON, K0E 1R0, or E-Mail: ont.sli@pc.gc.ca Tel: (613) 923-5261

Ask for the publication "A Paddler's Guide to Exploring the 1000 Islands and St. Lawrence Islands National Park."

Canadian Recreational Canoeing Association

In 1971 the CRCA was created by a number of recreational canoeing enthusiasts who perceived the need for a national body to co-ordinate the efforts of non-competitive canoeing and kayaking. The Association now acts as the national office for ten provincial, three territorial associations and 2.3 million recreational paddlers.

The mandate of the CRCA is organized into four basic areas: safety, environmental ethics, heritage and information services and programmes. Seminars, workshops and guest speakers on many topics relating to outdoor recreation activities are presented throughout the year. Each summer the CRCA hosts the Canadian Canoe Symposium on the third weekend of August.

Some of their key operations include the promotion of safe paddling, establishing national courses and certification programmes for the public, distribution of the Canoeists Code of Ethics on environmental issues, management of Bill Mason Memorial Scholarship Fund, helping to expand Heritage River Systems and participate in waterway management discussions.

KANAWA - Canada's Paddling Magazine, KANAWA is for anyone who loves to paddle. It is the best source of information, inspiration and guidance for everyone thinking about a Canadian paddling adventure. It is perfect for anyone who enjoys wonderful expedition stories, great outdoor photography and discovering new possibilities for adventure. KANAWA also features important environmental and safety issues. This full colour magazine is published four times a year. Subscriptions are available.

The Canadian Recreational Canoe Association Headquarters is located in the Rideau Outdoor Centre in Merrickville. The rustic timberframe building features a unique store containing hundreds of books and videos on Canada's breathtaking wilderness, an art and photography exhibit and a display of historic canoes, kayaks and paddles. Canoe and kayak rentals are available by the hour and by the day. For paddling information, please contact the Canadian Recreational Canoeing Association, P.O. Box 398, 446 Main St. W., Merrickville, Ontario, K0G 1N0 Tel: 613-269-2910, Fax: 613-269-2908, Toll Free: 1-888-252-6292, e-mail: info@paddlingcanada.com or visit their website at www.paddlingcanada.com

Rideau by Trail

Trail near Hartwells
Photo Credit: Steve Weir, Rideau Canal, Parks Canada

Lockstation Walking Tours
Rideau Trail ~ Cataraqui Trail
Cycling the Rideau

Lockstation Walking Tours

*A*n abundance of wonderful trails exist along the Rideau Canal Corridor. Interpretive brochures are available at most lockstations where trails are featured. The Friends of the Rideau and Parks Canada make these brochures easily available to you. These organizations work together in establishing and maintaining trails, providing benches, picnic tables and trail markers for your information and enjoyment.

Jones Falls Lockstation Walking Tour- Site attractions here include: the operating blacksmith shop, Sweeney House, the stone arch dam - a remarkable engineering feat, Basin Trail- a rugged terrain adventure and more.

The Ottawa Locks Walking Tour- Site attractions here include: The Sappers Bridge, Blacksmith Shop, Commissariat Building - home of Bytown Museum, Majors Hill Park, the famous Chateau Laurier and Parliament Hill. This is an historical and metropolitan walking tour.

The Burritts Rapids Tip to Tip Trail is an easy walk with a round trip distance of 4 km. It will take you through the village of Burritts Rapids. Trail markers will highlight features important in Rideau Canal construction.

The **Merrickville Depot to Dam Trail** takes visitors from the Friends of the Rideau retail outlet and interpretive centre-*The Depot*, to the tip of the old cut stone dam at the west end of the embankment that separates the original channel of the Rideau River from the canal cut. The trail heads out along this embankment and provides the visitor with interesting views of heritage and nature. The interpretive brochure, available at The Depot, not only guides your way but informs and delights.

Photo Credit: Steve Weir, Rideau Canal, Parks Canada   *Bicycle at Hartwells*

- In Ottawa both **Hogs Back** (Lock 11-12) and **Hartwells** (Locks 9-10) offer self guiding trails through beautiful greenspaces in the heart of the city.

- Follow the trail offered at Poonamalie (Lock 32).

- There is a lookout and trail at Upper Beveridges (Lock 33).

- Self-guiding trails can be found on **Colonel By Island.**

- There is also a self-guiding trail at **Smiths Falls Combined Lockstation** (Lock 29a).

The Depot, Merrickville

Hiking the Rideau

Hiking the Rideau Corridor is a great way to enjoy the scenery and view the sights. The two longest trails are the Rideau Trail, extending from Kingston to Ottawa and the Cataraqui Trail, part of the Trans-Canada Trail system, extending from Strathcona to Smiths Falls. There are also dozens of other smaller trails, located in parks and conservation areas along the system.

Rideau Trail (200 km one way, 300 km including loops & side trails) - the Rideau Trail is the longest trail in the area, extending from Kingston to Ottawa. It is a hiking only trail with some cross country skiing and snowshoeing. It is maintained by the Rideau Trail Association. The association publishes a Rideau Trail Guidebook which is an excellent resource, a full description of the trail including fold-out 1:50,000 maps with the trail clearly marked. Website: www.rideautrail.org/ Phone: 613-545-0823

Cataraqui Trail (104 km) The Cataraqui Trail extends from Strathcona to Smiths Falls. It is part of the Trans-Canada trail system and follows an old railway bed, so it is a very easy hike. Full details, including a trail map, are available on the Cataraqui Trail Website: www.rideau-info.com/cattrail Phone:613-546-4228

The Northern Trails (Ottawa to Smiths Falls)

Chapman Mills Conservation Area (1.5 km): Located on Prince of Wales Drive in Ottawa. Features walkways and boardwalks along natural shoreline and wetlands. Website: www.rideauvalley.on.ca/careas/chapman Phone:1-800-267-3504

Marlborough Forest - on County Road 6 west of North Gower and north of Burritts Rapids. This forested area is owned by the City of Ottawa. There are many trails and abandoned roadways. Part of the Rideau Trail also runs through this forest. Website: members.rogers.com/larry.neily/marlboro.htm

Baxter Conservation Area: Located on Regional Road 13 (Dilworth Drive) off Highway 16, south of Kars. It features swimming, hiking and year round programs. It has a 5 km walking trail, an Interpretive Centre, marsh boardwalk, toilets, a beach, change house, small boat launch, picnic tables and a picnic shelter. Website:

www.rideauvalley.on.ca/careas/baxter Phone: 1-800-267-3504.

Rideau River Provincial Park (3.5 km): Located on County Road 5 just across the Rideau River from Kemptville. It has a 3.5 km walking trail along the shore of the Rideau River. Website: www.rideauvalley.on.ca/careas/baxter Phone:1-800-267-3504.

Tip to Tip Trail (4 km): Located at Burritts Rapids, the starting point is the Burritts Rapids Lockstation on Rideau River Road (Cty Rd. 23). The trail takes you along Burritts Rapids Island and there are interpretive stops along the trail.

The Southern Trails -(Kingston to Smiths Falls)

Little Cataraqui Creek Conservation Area: Located 2 km north of Hwy. 401 on Division St. (County Road 10), Kingston. Offers 5 trails of varying lengths, plus picnic tables, washrooms, canoe rentals and an outdoor centre. Website: www.cataraquiregion.on.ca/lands/little-cat.htm Phone: (613) 546-4228

Frontenac Provincial Park (150 km): Located on Salmon Lake Road, north of Sydenham, the park features 12 different trails ranging in length from 1.5 to 21 kilometres. Many are wilderness trails, sights include waterfalls, beaver ponds, lakes and abandoned homesteads and mica mines. Part of the Rideau Trail crosses the southern side of the park. Website: www.ontarioparks.com/english/fron-hiking.html Phone:1-888-ONT-PARK (668-7275)

Charleston Lake Provincial Park (30 km): Located on County Road 3 south of Lyndhurst, this park features 6 different trails ranging in length from 1.6 to 10 kilometres. Sights include various forms of wildlife habitat, shorelines, wetlands, pioneer homesteads and lake viewpoints. Website: www.ontarioparks.com/english/char-hiking.html Phone: 1-888-ONT-PARK (668-7275)

Foley Mountain Conservation Area (6 km): located near Westport, off County Road 10, it offers swimming, group camping, hiking, educational programs. It also has a 6 km walking trail, an Interpretive Centre, toilets, beach, change house, picnic tables and a picnic shelter. Website: www.rideauvalley.on.ca/careas/foley Phone:613-273-3255

Mill Pond Conservation Area (15 km): located on Briton-Houghton Bay Road, off Highway 15 between Portland and Lombardy. Offers natural habitat and a seasonal sugarbush program. It also has a 15 km walking trail, a seasonal Interpretive Centre, toilets, small boat launch, picnic tables and a picnic shelter. Website: www.rideauvalley.on.ca/careas/millpond Phone:1-800-267-3504

Murphys Point Provincial Park (20 km): Located 19 km south of Perth on County Road 21, the park has 5 hiking trails ranging in length from 1 to 5.5 kilometres. Sights include interpretive displays, beaver ponds, Silver Queen Mica Mine, viewscapes of Big Rideau Lake, beaches and mixed forest. In addition, 6.5 km of the Rideau Trail traverses the park. Website: www.ontarioparks.com/english/murp-hiking.html Phone: 1-888-ONT-PARK (668-7275)

Tour the Silver Queen Mine at Murphy's Point Provincial Park

Perth Wildlife Reserve (4 km): Off County Road 1 between Perth and Rideau Ferry. It features a wildlife area, including an overlook of the Tay Marsh. It provides for goose habitat with a goose landing zone and features a 4 km walking trail. It also has toilets. Website: www.rideauvalley.on.ca/careas/perth Phone:1-800-267-3504

Historic Village Walking Tours

Available for: Delta, Perth, Elgin, Portland, Merrickville, Newboro, Smiths Falls, Manotick, Westport. See maps and line drawings on www.rideau-info.com Brochures are available in most community info stations and are designed to acquaint visitors and residents with our rich local history and to illustrate the variety of architectural features that appear as each village matured.

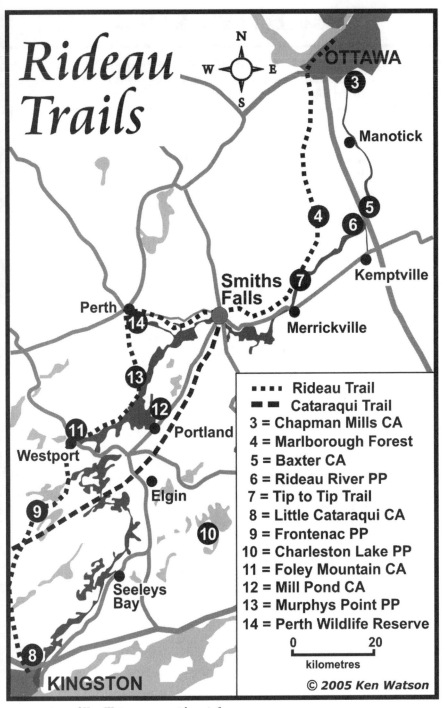

map courtesy of Ken Watson - www.rideau-info.com

Cycling the Rideau

The **Ontario East Cycling Map** is available from many tourist outlets and details bike routes throughout eastern Ontario. Bikes are not permitted on the Rideau Trail but the Cataraqui trail is a 'shared use' trail open to hikers and cyclists. Many secondary roads in the Rideau Canal corridor make perfect bike trails. Bicycles can be rented in the big cities of course and some locations in the smaller villages offer bike rentals including a few B&Bs along the way. Bring your own bikes on the top of your car or strapped to your boat. Or better yet rent a bike at **Cyco's Bike Rentals** - 5 Hawthorne Rd., Ottawa Phone: 613-567-8180.

Information about **Cycle Rideau Lanark** can be found by calling 613-283-5810. Call Lanark County Tourist Association for info about cycling in and around Perth 613-267-4200.

A fabulous bike tour offered by the Ottawa Bicycle Club is the **Rideau Lakes Cycle Tour** usually taking place over 2 days in June. This annual event offers a up close chance to enjoy the picturesque ride from Ottawa to Kingston and back. It has attracted more than 1000 cyclists each year since 1971. For tour information contact the Ottawa Bicycle Club, P.O. Box 4298 Station E,Ottawa, ON, K1S 5B3, Canada 613-230-1064 or 613-230-9504www.ottawabicycleclub.ca.

For information on the summer-long Rideau Lakes Cycling Tours, call: 1-888-804-4696 or visit website: www.rideaulakescycling.ca

In Ottawa there is a Super Sunday Bikeday program allowing participants to walk, inline skate, bike, or use their wheelchairs with no traffic trouble. Every Sunday during the summer 65 kms of National Capital area parkways are closed to motorized traffic.

For cyclists visiting Ottawa or boaters using bicycles to tour the Ottawa area, Supervised Bicycle Parking Facilities are available throughout the Summer on William St. in the ByWard Market. As well OC Transpo, the Ottawa City Bus service, offers 'Rack & Roll' a new project to help you to participate in the Bike & Ride program. This transport service helps cyclists to enjoy the regions bike routes and paths without having to negotiate street traffic to get there. For information about this program call OC Transpo 613-741-4390.

Fishing Guide

photo credit: Rideau Canal, Parks Canada Archive

Rideau Hot Spots
Tips & Techniques
Regulations

ℱishing Guide

ℱishing is the ideal recreational boating activity because you can do it with the whole family or you can do it alone when you need some peace and quiet.

As with most boating activities, there are a few important things to keep in mind. For example, a good angler should show respect for private property, public waterways and the rights of other anglers. One way of showing this respect is to leave the environment as clean as it was before you got there.

Another thing to keep in mind is the need to put safety first in the use of fishing equipment and in your enjoyment of the sport. Anglers with some experience should always share their safety knowledge with those who are just learning to fish.

As well as sharing safety, there is a tradition among anglers of sharing their skills with beginners. Many a young person has become an enthusiastic angler because someone took the time to share his or her experience.

Beginners need to know about the importance of fishing regulations, conservation, how to avoid damaging the natural habitat, and last but not least, beginners need to learn respect for fish in general, before and after catching them.

The Rideau provides many excellent fishing opportunities. Although renown for its prolific and high quality bass fishing, the Rideau will also provide fishing enjoyment for those going after other species including Lake Trout, Black Crappie, Northern Pike, Muskellunge, and Walleye. If you have young kids with you, get a hook, bobber and bucket of worms (available from all bait stores in the region) and be prepared for an endless catch of Sunfish.

Fishing boat at rest, The Opinicon dock

There are many rules and regulations to keep in mind, ask the Ministry of Natural Resources for a copy of the Ontario Sport Fishing Regulations Summary.

For information on fishing rules and regulations, licenses and special events for anglers contact one of the following organizations:

Ontario Ministry of Natural Resources   1-800-667-1940

Ontario Federation of Anglers and Hunters   1-800-353-4005

Northern Ontario Tourist Outfitters   (705) 472-5552

Resorts Ontario   www.resorts-ontario.com   1-800-363-7227

Ontario Family Fishing Weekend Event Information Line
     1-800-667-1940

Ontario's Conservation Areas   www.out-there.com/ca00ont.htm

For additional information write, phone or visit the Ministry of Natural Resources:

> Ministry of Natural Resources
> 300 Water Street, P.O. Box 7000,
> Peterborough, ON, K9J 8M5
> General Inquiry -   1-800-667-1940

Natural Resources Information Centre

> in Toronto   1-800-667-1840
> French Inquiry   1-800-667-1840

It is possible to download the Sportfishing Regulations from the MNR web-site at www.mnr.gov.on.ca

Here are some of the key regulations for the Rideau region. Always confirm with the Ministry of Natural Resources in case of change and be sure to read regulations carefully.

For the **Fishing Season** on the Rideau

	Southern/Northern Regions - Central Region	
Bass* (Largemouth & Smallmouth)	June 26 to November 30	June 26 to Oct. 15
Walleye (Pickerel)	Jan 1 to March 15	Jan 1 to Feb 28
	May 8 to Dec. 31	May 8 to Dec 31
Northern Pike	Jan 1 to March 31	Jan 1 to Feb 28
	May 8 to Dec.31	May 10 to Dec 31
Lake Trout	June 4 (1st Sat) to Sept. 8	June 4 to Sept. 8
Muskellunge	June 4 to Nov. 30	June 4 to Nov. 30

Please Note: *It is illegal to fish for Bass (or any other fish) before the season opens, even if you plan to release. It is especially damaging to bass during the spawning and rearing season in the spring. If adult bass are taken away from their nests the young are left unprotected and subject to predation.*

There is a year-round ban on fishing with live or dead lake herring (cisco) as bait.

Catch & Possession Limits

Standard License

Species	Limits
Bass (large & smallmouth)	6 per day
	(central reg. min size 30cm/11.8in)
Northern Pike	6 per day
Walleye (Pickerel)	6 per day
	(central reg. min. size 5cm/13.8in)
Lake Trout	2 per day
Crappie	30 per day
Whitefish	25 per day
Muskellunge	1 per day Possession limit 2
	(min size 112cm/44in)

There are no seasonal or catch limits on yellow perch.

Conservation License

Species	Limits
Bass (large & smallmouth)	2 per day
	(central reg. min size 30cm/11.8in)
Northern Pike	2 per day
Walleye (Pickerel)	2 per day
	(central reg. min. size 5cm/13.8in)
Lake Trout	1 per day
Crappie	10 per day
Whitefish	12 per day

Note: The catch limit is the number of fish you are allowed to catch and keep in one day. Fish eaten for shore meals are included in the daily catch limit. The possession limit refers to the number of fish allowed on hand in storage or transit. With the exception of Musky the possession limit is the same as the catch limit.

Fishing Licenses

For Ontario Residents a Resident Sport Fishing License or a Resident Conservation License is required. An Outdoors Card or a temporary permit and card application form are necessary in order to purchase a License. Prices including GST are listed below.

Outdoor Card plus 3 year resident Sport Fishing Tag -	$ 72.00
Outdoor Card plus 3 year resident Conservation Fishing Tag -	$ 45.00
Outdoors Card (valid for 3 years) -	$ 6.00
1 year Resident Seasonal License Tag -	$ 22.00
1 year Resident Conservation License Tag -	$ 13.00
Resident 1-day License -	$ 12.00

You do not require a license if you are under 18, over 65 or disabled.

*This information is subject to change, please contact MNR for current fees/dates/limits www.gov.on.ca

For Canadian Residents residing outside Ontario prices are the same as above without the disabled exemption.

Anyone who is not a resident of Ontario or Canada is considered a non-resident. A Non-Resident Sport Fishing License allows you to fish with a hook and line. Those under 18 may fish with a licensed adult. Prices including GST are listed below.

Non-resident Seasonal License - $ 61.00

Non-resident Conservation License - $ 37.00

Non-resident 7-Day License - $ 39.00

Non-resident 7-Day Conservation License - $ 23.00

Non-resident License for a Member of an Organized Camp (per child) $ 4.00

There is no exemption for non-residents over 65.

Fishing out of season, without a License or exceeding catch limits are offenses under the Game and Fish Act with penalties of up to $25,000. Poaching is stealing. Please report illegal fishing activities to Crime stoppers at Canada Wide call toll free: 1-800-222-TIPS (8477)

Fishing Boats can be rented at many locations, see the boat rentals page. Tackle and Bait shops are easily found.

A great way to support responsible fishing in Ontario is to join the Ontario Federation of Anglers and Hunters. They can be reached at:
The Ontario Federation of Anglers and Hunters
P.O. Box 2800
Peterborough, Ontario
K9J 8L5
Tel: (705) 748-6324
Fax: (705) 748-9577

The following Rideau Fish descriptions are from Ken Watson's Rideau Information website. For more details on Rideau Fishing visit the **Fishing** *section on* ***www.rideau-info.com.***

𝓑𝓪𝓼𝓼

$\mathcal{B}$ oth largemouth and smallmouth bass occur on the Rideau, although largemouth predominate. Bass are members of the sunfish family. At the turn of the century, the Rideau lakes, particularly the southern lakes (Sand, Opinicon, Indian, Clear, and Newboro), were renown as the best bass fishing spots in North America with catches of over 100 per day not uncommon. It still provides excellent opportunities for bass fishing, with many visitors coming to the region just to fish for bass.

Largemouth Bass prefer warmer waters than smallmouth. When fishing for Largemouth think "weedy cover". These are areas where baitfish abound and they attract largemouth bass. Bays with weeds and sunken logs, and a water depth of 5 to 15 feet make ideal largemouth bass habitat. During summer fishing season the best spot will be a point with a soft sandy bottom, containing reeds and weeds, adjacent to a soft bottom bay. The fish will have moved out of the bay after spawning, and will now spend most of the summer in and around the point.

Largemouth inhabit the whole of the Rideau from Kingston to Ottawa. Although the south central lakes (noted above) are the most renown for Largemouth they can be caught anywhere along the Rideau.

Deep notch

upper jaw extends beyond eye

dark lateral streak from head to tail

Large Mouth Bass is a scrapy fish. Fun to catch and delicate tasting. Average size is 2-3lbs can exceed 8lbs. Trolling, and still-fishing are the best ways to catch. Hint: find a quiet lake or channel with lots of shoals, submerged islands and stumps. At dusk and dawn they can be found close to shore in weed beds.

Small Mouth Bass

When fishing for Smallmouth Bass think "structure and crayfish". Crayfish like habitat with small (fist sized) broken rocks. Find an area like this adjacent to larger rocks (which provides cover for the bass) and you will be in smallmouth heaven. In rivers smallmouth tend to be concentrated near current breaking structures (rocks, islands, bends).

Smallmouth can be found throughout the Rideau, although not in the same numbers as Largemouth. Fishing structure (points, shoals, islands) in lakes such as Big Rideau and Upper Rideau will reward the angler with a smallmouth on the line.

dark blotches on sides and back

shallow notch

upper jaw does not extend beyond back of the eye

*Like the Largemouth Bass the **Smallmouth Bass** has an average size of 2-3 lbs. They too can be caught around shoals, deadwood and weedy areas using minnows or frogs.*

Walleye

The Walleye (also known as doré and sometimes erroneously called the **Yellow Pickerel**, which is actually a pike) is a member of the perch family. Their main food source are minnows and perch and they prefer the cooler waters that smallmouth like. Earlier in the season some will tend to stay in deep water, close to their source of baitfish, near emerging weed beds. Others will stay in deep water off mudflats where emerging insects form the main food source. As summer progresses, the walleye tend to school together and will follow the food source. This will include areas such as sunken islands and mid-lake humps. Similar to many species, fishing picks up in the fall, when food sources start to become scarcer and the fish become a bit more aggressive in their search for food.

Walleye can be found at various spots along the Rideau, including Clear and Newboro lakes and in the Rideau River at places like the dam at Burritt's Rapids and the dam at Black Rapids.

cloudy eye

fins separate with large black blotch on back of spinous fin

sharp teeth

Yellow Pickerel or Walleye is a popular game fish easily distinguished by its large opaque eyes. June bug spinners and non-lead jigs are good lures, if casting at river mouth. Hint: Slow trolling the deep waters later in the season when they are feeding from lake and river bottoms.

Lake Trout

ake Trout (a member of the char family), prefer clear cold water. They can be found in the deeper lakes of the Rideau. Trout feed on various types of baitfish (Alewife, Cisco, Smelt, Chubb, Sculpin). In spring, Lake Trout can be found close to shore but as the weather warms up, the trout will move deeper, staying in their preferred temperature range. They prefer to stay near drop-offs, ledges, and side slopes rather than the flat bottom areas of the lake. So look for such structures at a depth that their temperature range indicates. In summer this can be anywhere from 60 to 100 feet deep in the lake.

Lake Trout are relatively easy to find on the Rideau, but much harder to catch. Look for areas on your charts with water depths in excess of 60 feet. These include Big Rideau Lake, Indian Lake and parts of Dog Lake. Lake Trout take a long time to grow and mature so please strictly adhere to catch limits or if possible only catch and release, leaving the fish in the water for the enjoyment of others.

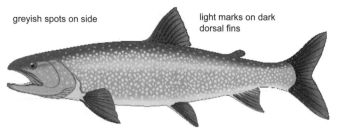

greyish spots on side

light marks on dark dorsal fins

lake trout with their deep-forked tail fin, are found in deep lakes and can be caught with flies, spinners or small live bait. They average 3-5 lbs. If you are after one of the big ones, you will need a wire line for depth.

Muskellunge and Northern Pike

𝒯he Muskellunge (or more properly the Maskinonge) and the Northern Pike are members of the same species, the pike family. They look very similar, an easy way to tell them apart is to count the sensory pores on the underside of the jaw (small holes that outline the jaw bone). Northern Pike have 9 to 11 of these pores while Muskie have 12 to 20. Another, though less accurate distinguishing feature is that the skin of a Northern Pike generally has light markings on a dark background while the skin of a muskie has dark markings on a light background.

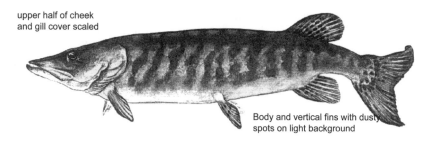

upper half of cheek and gill cover scaled

Body and vertical fins with dusty spots on light background

Muskellunge are commonly called Muskie and are a challenge to any good angler. Vertical bars on sides resemble the rippled sandy bottom of a lake. Averages 8-10lbs up to 30lbs. These are wily creatures, not easily caught. Hint: Fast trolling deepwater near weed beds is the best bet.

At one end of the fishing spectrum are those that consider pike a nuisance fish. At the other end are the tried and true Muskie fisherman who wouldn't fish for any other species. These fish are at the top of the freshwater food chain. The only predator of a mature pike or muskie is man.

Northern Pike can be found throughout the whole of the Rideau system from Kingston to Ottawa. Their diet consists mostly of baitfish such as perch, shiners, ciscoes and herring. They aren't too picky and are willing to eat most anything that moves through the water. In the spring and fall, pike tend to hang out near weedy bays and shoals. They prefer cooler water (see chart) and as summer approaches they will move into deeper, cooler water adjacent to their spring and fall forage areas. If the water gets too warm pike will stop feeding.

Muskies tend to hang out in the same types of places that Walleye do. In fact large Muskie will often stay near a school of Walleye, feeding on both the baitfish the Walleye eat and the Walleye themselves. Thus in summer you will find them generally suspended over deeper water near a slow taper shoal that Walleye prefer.

Pike are found throughout the Rideau with good pike fishing to be had in the Rideau River north of Smiths Falls (between Edmonds and Clowes locks) and near Chaffey's Lock. Muskie can be found in both the St. Lawrence and Ottawa Rivers and in the Rideau River near Black Rapids and between Nicholsons Lock and Burritts Rapids. Muskie are sensitive to fishing pressure so please take a camera along and practice catch and release fishing.

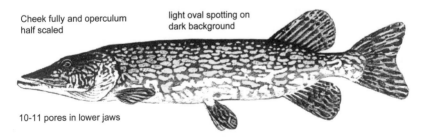

Cheek fully and operculum half scaled

light oval spotting on dark background

10-11 pores in lower jaws

Northern Pike average between 2-4 lbs and weigh up to 20lbs. Mouths resemble duck bills. Hint:find weed bed, 10 ft deep, cast away using minnow or lg spoon with wire leader (pike bite through nylon) Wait until bait is swallowed and fish has begun to move away.

On the Rideau you will find some great resorts that cater to anglers. To plan a Rideau fishing vacation consider the following:

Melody Lodge and Marina offers full service marina as well as barbeque facilities and picnic tables, public phone and data jack for laptop downloading. Fishing licenses and tackle are also available here. At Melody you will find cottages, seasonal and transient trailer sites with full service, campsites, seasonal and transient dockage, boat and motor rentals, gas, diesel, pump-out and a mini-store where you will find their famous ice cream. They host an 'Annual Friendly Bass Tournament', for trailer residents and guests staying in the cottages or camping. Contact them at Melody Lodge and Marina, 4328 Melody Lodge Road, R.R.3, Seeley's Bay Ontario K0H 2N0 Phone: 1-888-MELODY-1 or (613) 387-3497 Visit their website at www.melody-lodge.ca

The Opinicon Resort Hotel has an interesting history. Originally called Camp Easy when established in the 1890s it was later known as the Openacon Club, an exclusive fishing resort. The main part of the building is more than 130 years old. In 1922 the property was purchased by the current owner's family and its been a haven to tourists and anglers ever since. The Opinicon offers American Plan accommodations in either hotel or cottages, fine dining and recreation as well as docking facilities. Call 613-359-5233 Fax 613-359-6527 or visit their website ate www.theopiniconresorthotel.com

Hotel Kenney is a fine old country inn, built in 1877 and is still operated by the Kenney family. Here you'll find great accommodations, fishing trips that can be arranged with an experienced guide, boat rentals and marina facilities. A convenience store, newsstand and laundromat are on site, along with a coffee shop, and dining room with an excellent wine cellar. A lovely gift shop is located next to the lobby. To reserve or plan a guided fishing trip call 1-866-KENNEYS or visit their website www.hotelkenney.com

perch

Rideau by Road

Road Tours
Accommodation Listings

Road Tours

Travelling the Rideau by road offers a multitude of opportunities to sight-see and explore. Those who wish to make use of the Rideau's waters for fishing may choose to trailer their fishing boat around and camp at various campsites, stay at B&B's or get right into the fishing spirit by checking out the area's famous fishing lodges. Perhaps you wish to carry your canoe on top of the car or van and pop it in the water wherever you fancy, stay at a local inn, camp at a lock-site or visit a family resort. Perhaps taking a boat tour and enjoying the history and beauty of the canal while letting someone else steer the boat is more your style. Maybe boating has nothing to do with it and you'd prefer to drive leisurely through the small towns along the Rideau Corridor taking in the history and visiting attractions and shops, and enjoying the food all from the security of dry land. Whatever your pleasure the Rideau has got it.

The Rideau Canal itself is accessible by car at most lockstations, Hwy 15 from Kingston will get you to most access roads. Lockstations are clearly marked on highways. It is approximately two hours from Kingston to Ottawa without stopping, but we'd recommend a few days to take in as many of the sights as possible.

St. Lawrence St., Merrickville

Rideau Driving Tours

Ken Watson's wonderful web-site offers a variety of Rideau Driving Tours, one is sure to appeal to you. The details can be found on www.rideau-info.com. Your choices include, **Rideau Heritage Tours** - for North, South, Central regions, **Shopping Tours**, **Eco Tours**, **Maple Tours**, **Fall Colour Tour** and **Picnic Tours**.

Here we have provided some simple tours, involving short drives, great towns and lots to explore. Use a current Ontario Road Map to help you find your way and choose alternate routes.

North Rideau Tour

OTTAWA TO MERRICKVILLE

Begin your journey from Ottawa to Manotick - Take County Road 73 south to Rideau Valley Drive and follow this to the village of Manotick. Watson's Mill in the Dickinson Square Conservation Area is located on Mill Street, watch for the conservation area signs. Built in 1860, it is one of the best preserved mills in Ontario. Mills were present all along the Rideau system. Their purposes were many and around them villages flourished.

Next to the mill is an interesting memorial to Canadian and Allied Forces, you'll find names etched on stones leading to the Mill. Stop for a picnic across the mill bridge. Quaint boutiques and delightful eateries can be found in Manotick, take a stroll down Main Street before you go.

From Manotick take the leisurely scenic route south on C.R. 19 to C. R. 43 to Merrickville - In Merrickville look for the historic Blockhouse just to the west of the main intersection in town. A public parking area can be found near the Blockhouse. Merrickville was founded in 1795 by William Merrick, a millwright from

Behind Watson's Mill, Manotick

Massachusetts, who set up a mill on the Rideau River at the site of the falls. The mill is long gone, but the community of Merrickville continues to thrive.

Your first stop will be *The Depot*, located on the waterfront just a bit west of the Blockhouse. Run by Friends of the Rideau, it offers a great deal of information, books, souvenirs and knowledgable staff. After you have browsed *The Depot*, and perhaps had a boat tour of the Bird Sanctuary, head over to the Blockhouse Museum. Then cross over the bridge and visit the old industrial mill complex, lots of stonework and machinery dating from the 19th century. The village of Merrickville will consume your day. Explore the fantastic array of unique boutiques and specialty shops, like *Mirick's Landing* just across Main Street from the Blockhouse. Stop at one of many dining establishments, from fast food to gourmet dining rooms. When you are finally ready to continue on your way, pick up a quick snack for the road at *'Round the Corner Bakeshop* and head out of town.

Blockhouse Museum, Merrickville   *Photo Credit: Steve Weir, Rideau Canal, Parks Canada*

When you are back in the car head over the swing bridge and take C.R. 2 to Burritts Rapids. In 1793, three Loyalist Burritt brothers, led by Stephen Burritt, established themselves in Marlborough Township and founded the settlement of Burritts Rapids. Turn right at the sign to Burritts Rapids, notice the beautiful church on the left, then go into the village of Burritts Rapids. The village itself is on a small island. Stop and have a look at the bridge on the south end of town. The first bridge across the Rideau was built here in 1824. The present steel truss swing bridge dates to 1897. The bridge is opened by turning a crank in the pivot at one end of the bridge. Counter weights and a set of roller wheels mounted on a circular track underneath allow the bridge to be swung with little effort. From here cross the bridge and head east on to River Road, the lockstation is 1km down on the left. It is a quiet spot with a great walking trail. Enjoy a snack and watch the boats lock through before you head back to Ottawa.

It is a scenic drive back.- Continue east along River Road to C.R. 44, turn north crossing over the Rideau to C.R. 5. Keep heading north to North Gower and then into Ottawa.

Central Rideau Tour

SMITHS FALLS - PORTLAND - PERTH
SIDE ROUTE: NEWBORO - WESTPORT

egin your journey in Smiths Falls - You may have already spent a day enjoying the many attractions including Railway Museum, the Bascule Bridge National Historic Site, the Rideau Canal Museum, Heritage House Museum, the Hershey Chocolate Factory, as well as the lovely parks and interesting shops.

From Smiths Falls to Portland on Hwy. 15, through Lombardy - take the detour into Rideau Ferry on C.R. 1 for some antiquing or stop for a bite at the restaurant on the right across the Rideau Ferry Bridge. Return to Hwy. 15 and head south to Portland. Stop at the Rideau Lakes Visitor Info booth just off the highway and find out about local sites to see. Take a boat tour on Big Rideau Lake, if you so desire or continue your journey on Hwy. 15 to Crosby. Here you may decide whether to take the scenic and delightful side trip to Newboro and Westport, around Upper Rideau Lake or to Cross at Narrows Lock station and head directly to Perth on (Narrows Lock Road) C.R. 14. It is a leisurely drive from the Narrows Lock back to Perth. The drive to Westport on C.R. 42 is long but definitely worth the time.

Visitor Welcome Centre, Westport

From Crosby take C.R. 42 west to Newboro. Newboro offers some great shopping opportunities. Continue on to Westport where you will find many eateries and delightful boutiques to enjoy. Stop in at the Welcome Centre on Spring Street for walking tours and local highlights. Once you have had your fill here, hop back in the car and head north on C.R. 10 to Perth.

Code's Mill, Perth

In Perth an abundance of dining choices from fast food to gourmet cuisine can be found. Quaint shops, book stores, boutiques, groceries and more are all found in this full service town. Stroll down main street and browse, visit the farmer's market, relax and dine at a quaint outdoor café. Perth is a truly beautiful town enjoy a pleasant stop or picnic at Stewart Park; Code's Mill across the road offers great food choices and some unique shopping. It has every amenity for visitors and provides a pleasant atmosphere.

Most of the original homes and buildings are still standing and many of them have been restored, as a walk down the tree-lined streets of the downtown core will prove. Since many of the settlers were Scottish stonemasons, the buildings were extremely well-constructed and a walking tour is most interesting. A brochure with self-guided walking tours can be picked up at the Visitor Information Centre at the Old Fire Hall on Herriot Street near Gore.

South Rideau Tour

KINGSTON TO CHAFFEY'S LOCK

From Kingston take Hwy. 15 north to Kingston Mills - Departing from City Hall, drive north on Ontario Street, over the bridge and crossing the mouth of the Cataraqui and entrance to the Rideau Canal, past Royal Military College and Old Fort Henry, and turn left at the lights (at the top of the hill) onto Hwy. 15. Take Hwy. 15 over Hwy. 401 and the railway tracks then turn left following the signs for Kingston Mills. Kingston Mills is the first lockstation at the southern end of the Rideau. It features the beautiful masonry stonework of all the locks, expansive lawns, and one of four blockhouses along the

Rideau. Take a tour through the Anglin interpretive centre to find out why and how the locks were constructed. Watch the locks in action and ask the canal staff for details on how they work.

From Kingston Mills continue on Hwy. 15 north, turn right onto Hwy. 33 to Lyndhurst - In Lyndhurst you will cross over one of the earliest stone bridges built in the region. The present stone bridge was built in 1856. From Lyndhurst take C.R. 2 to C.R. 42 and turn left to Delta. Many of the communities along the Rideau got their start by being near fast running water, the ideal location for a mill. The Old Stone Mill in Delta, circa 1810, is the only stone grist mill in Canada to be designated a National Historic Site. After your tour of the mill, pick up the "Walking Tour of Delta" brochure for more things to do and see in Delta.

From here continue north on C.R. 42 to Forfar and the Forfar Cheese Factory. It is at the west end of town, just after C.R. 42 makes a sharp turn to the left. Pick up some samples of Eastern Ontario's finest cheese for your continuing journey.

From Forfar take C.R. 42 to Crosby, then Hwy. 15 south to C.R. 9 and Chaffey's Lock. This tiny community hosts a lovely lock, a swing bridge, a grist mill turned antique shop, a defensible lockmaster's house turned museum, and the historic Opinicon Resort Hotel. Nearby is Cedars Art Studio, and the Chaffey's Lock Memory Wall both are well worth a visit. If at all possible enjoy a fabulous meal at The Opinicon, originally built as a private residence for John Chaffey in 1868.

Chaffey's Mill, now a quaint antique shop

The drive from Chaffey's Lock to Kingston is on Hwy. 15 south. It will take about 50 minutes. If you choose to take a more scenic yet less travelled (gravel) road, consider crossing the bridge at Chaffey's Lock to CRT. 10, then south to Kingston.

Where to Stay:

As you are planning your trip to the Rideau you will need to know what accommodations are available and where they can be found. Campsites, B&Bs, Inns, Resorts and Hotels can all be found along the Rideau Corridor. Call for reservations and information. Don't forget about lockstation camping available to those who arrive by foot, boat or bike.

Kingston

Ambassador Resort Hotel - 613-548-3605/1-800-267-7880

Best Western Fireside Inn - 613-549-2211

Comfort Inn By Journey's End 613-549-5550

Days Inn Kingston Hotel & Convention Cntr. 613-546-3661

Four Points Hotel & Suites Sheraton - 613-544-4434/1-888-478-4333

Green Acres Inn - 613-546-1796

Holiday Inn Waterfront Kingston - 613-549-8400/1-800-465-4329

Howard Johnson Hotel - 613-549-6300

Kingston Motels (east)613-546-6674 (west)613-547-7979

Knights Inn 613-531-8929

Lord Nelson 613-542-2883

Peachtree Inn - 613-546-4411

Ramada Plaza Hotel Harbourfront 613-549-8100

Rest Inn Motel - 613-546-6616

Super 8 Motel - 613-542-7395

Travelodge Hotel - 613-546-4233

Limestone City B&Bs -

Absolute Location B&B -613-545-1543

A Stone's Throw B&B - 613-544-6089

Alexander Henry B&B - 613-542-2261

B&B Frontenac Street - 613-549-7059

Bon Accord B&B 613-540-2378

Casablanca B&B 613-546-2011

Chart House B&B - 613-546-9026

Dwntwn Kingston B&B 613-544-9919

Frontenac Club B&B 613-547-6167

Green Woods B&B 613-544-1922

O'Brien House B&B 613-545-1741

Riverview B&B - 613-546-7707

Rosa's B&B 613-546-2008

Rosemount B&B - 613-531-8844

The Queens Inn 613-546-0429

Yellow Corner Cottage B&B -613-547-8079

Lake Ontario Park 613-542-6574

Rideau Acres Conference Facilities (Hwy 15) 613-546-2711

Seeley's Bay

Seeley's Bay Bay Motel Family Resort (613)387-3800

Melody Lodge & Marina, on Cranberry Lake - cottages, seasonal and transient trailer sites with full service, campsites, seasonal and transient dockage, boat and motor rentals, gas, diesel, pump-out and a mini-store where you will find their famous ice cream R.R.#3, 4328 Melody Lodge Rd., Seeley's Bay K0H 2N0 (888) MELODY-1 (613) 387-3497 www.melodylodge.ca

Rideau Breeze Marina, Cottages,
(613)387-3100
Sunny Acres Resort & Cottages -
(613)387-3379 Fax:(613)387-1052
Cranberry Lake Cottages -(613)387-1075
Shangri-La Marina, Lodge and
Campground, (613) 359-5774
Lakeside Bed & Breakfast (613)387-3806
Windrift Bed & Breakfast, (613)353-7378
Heron Point Bed & Breakfast
(613)387-1093
email: heronpoint@seeleysbay.com
Burnt Hills Lodge - 613-387-3527
Cranberry Park - 613-387-3275
Elm Lodge - 613-387-3424
Knapp's Brass Point Camping -
613-387-3912
Camp Brylene - 613-387-3468
Pleasantview Cottages - 613-387-3335
Rest Inn Overnite Camping 613-387-3121
Robert Hogan Enterprises(campground &
cottages) -613-387-3432
Top o' the Hill Bed & Breakfast -
613-387-3931
Windrift Bed & Breakfast - 613-353-7378
The Bay Motel - 613-387-3800
Moore's Cottages - 613-387-3442
Lakeside B&B - 613-387-3806

Jones Falls

Hotel Kenny Lock Road, Jones Falls, On
K0G 1E0 613-359-5500
1-866-KENNEYS www.hotelkenny.com
- located on Whitefish Lake beside Jones
Falls locks this lovely historic resort was
built in 1877. Main dining room with
excellent wine cellar with a fine selection
of lagers and ales from around the world.
A full service coffee shop is also open all
day.

HOTEL KENNY
A FINE OLD FAMILY RESORT
KENNY....SINCE 1877

Shangri-La Campground and Lodge -
613-359-5774

Elgin
*Leeds & Grenville B&B Association -
613-273-7848
Battam's Camp (cottages) - 613-359-5566
Casey's Camps - 613-359-5574
Lloyd's Cottages 613-359-5709
Sand Lake Campground (cottages) -
613-359-6361
Green Valley B&B - 613-359-5735
Pine Glen Lodge - 613-359-1060

Delta
Denault Mansion Country Inn -
613-928-2588
Lower Beverly Lake Park - 613-928-2881

Chaffey's Locks
The Opinicon 18 rooms and 30 cottages
on Opinicon Lake next to Chaffey's Lock. -
613-359-5233
www.theopiniconresorthotel.com

THE OPINICON
RESORT HOTEL

Indian Lake Campground -
613-359-5779
Davis Cottages - 613-359-6175
Dorothy's Fishing Lodge - 613-359-5116
Green Valley Cottages & Trailer Camp -
613-359-5799
Pine Glen Lodge - 613-359-1060
Simmons Lodge - 613-359-5811
Skycroft Campsites & Cottages -
1-877-359-5491

Sun on the Brow B&B - 613-359-5977

Newboro

Camp Mon O'Kel (cottages) - 613-272-2412

Caswell's Rental House - 315-597-5140

Clear Lake Cottages - 613-272-2745

The Poplars Resort - 613-272-2345

Pritchard's Cottages - 613-272-2564

Stirling Lodge - 613-272-2435

Swallows Cottages - 613-272-2516

Stagecoach Inn - 613-272-2900

Newboro House - B&B - 613-272-3181

Westport

Cobblestones Resort/Retreat 613- 273-5950
www.cobblestones.on.ca/

The Cove Country Inn - 613-273-3636
1-888-COVE-INN www.coveinn.com

A Bit of Gingerbread Bed & Breakfast - 613-273-7848

Brash's Camp - 613-273-3260

Grandpa Sach's - 613-273-7224

Howard's Cottages - 613-273-2855

Lilly's Cottages - 613-721-0080

McParland Cottages - 613-273-3281

Michaels Olde Frontenac Landing(cottages) 613-273-5294

Pine Haven Cottages & Campsites - 613-273-5365

Scott's Cottages & Campgrounds - 613-273-2880

Sunnyside Campground - 613-273-3124

Upper Rideau Resort - 613-273-7224

Westport Tent & Trailer Park
613-273-2013

Whitehouse Tent & Trailer Park - 613-273-5526

Wolfe Lake Cottages - 613-273-5491

Woodview Cove Campground - 613-273-3002

Arbuckle's Rideau View Bed & Breakfast - 613-273-4789

Deerwood Farm B&B - 613-273-4412

Loon Lake B&B - 613-273-2372

Fielding House Bed & Breakfast - 613-273-2661

New Beginnings Bed & Breakfast - 613-273-6063

Stepping Stone Country Heritage B&B Inn - 613-273-3806

Green Shingle Lodge - 613-273-5303

Nordlaw Lodge - 613-273-2920

Westport Station Motel - 613-273-3627

Kilpatrick House B&B - 613-273-2337

The Millpond - 613-273-2866

Spring Street B&B - 613-273-5427

The Village House B&B - 613-273-3663

Lakewood Crossing B&B - 613-273-4444

Narrow's Lock

Narrow's Lock Campground - 613-272-3401

Portland

Portland Bay Bed and Breakfast - (613) 272-0222
email: boattour@istar.ca
www.bbcanada.com/portlandbay

Cedar Cove Cottages - 613-272-2882

J&J's Big Rideau Resort - 613-272-2407

Len's Cove Marina - 613-272-2581
offers cottages

Miller's Little Rideau Lake Cottages - 613-272-2387

Murphys Point Provincial Park - 613-267-5060
167 regular campsites, 14 remote interior sites, some offer small craft dock facilities to campers.

Pritchard's Cottages - 613-272-2564

Rideau Mac Resort - 1-800-897-3331
613-272-2646

Seward's Cottages - 613-272-2409

Sunset on the Rideau - 613-272-2359

Waterways Campground - 613-272-2791

Gisela's B&B - 613-272-2246

Portland Bay B&B - 613-272-0222

Steamboat Landing B&B - 613-272-2992

Wendigo Acres Bed & Breakfast and
Riding Academy - 613-272-2597
Gallagher House Lakeside Country Inn -
613-272-2895

Rideau Ferry

Kerruish's Cottages - 613-267-6396
Maple Crest Motel & Cabins - 613-284-
4804

Perth

Lanark County Bed & Breakfast
Association - 613-257-8547
Last Duel Park - 613-267-3200
Jordan's Cottages - 613-267-1141
McCreary's Beach Resort - 613-267-4450
McCullough's Landing - 613-267-4310
Sandy Bay Cottages - 613-267-4783
Tay River Tent & Trailer Camp -
613-267-3955
Winton's Cottages - 613-267-2478
Chez Loraize Bed & Breakfast -
613-264-2846
Copeland B&B - 613-267-2355
Drummond House - 613-264-9175
Linden Meadow Farm - 613-259-2693
Maud's B&B - 613-267-5760
Perth Manor Heritage Inn Bed & Breakfast
- 613-264-0050
Rabb House - 613-264-0738
Rivendell Bed & Breakfast -
613-264-2742
Woodrow Farm - 613-267-1493
Aquarius Motel - 613-267-4261
Colonial House Motor Inn -
613-267-3660
Friendship Inn Perth - 613-267-3300/1-
800-4CHOICE
Perth Plaza Motel - 613-264-1022

Smiths Falls

Best Western Colonel By Inn -
613-284-0001/1-800-528-1234
Victoria Park - 613-283-5112
Cottages Unlimited - 613-284-0400

The Homestead - 613-283-1184
McEwen House Bed & Breakfast - 613-
284-1840
Dave's Holiday Motel - 613-283-7147
Fergusons Motel - 613-283-7220
Maple Leaf Motel - 613-283-3881
Comfort Inn - 613-283-5150
Roger's Motel - 613-283-5200
1-800-567-3642
Fasgath B&B - 613-283-5546
Homesteader Country Inn -
613-283-0223
Rideau Hotel - 613-283-3333

Merrickville

Sam Jakes Inn - Spa facilities, fine din-
ing, luxurious rooms. 613-269-3711
1-800-567-4667 www.samjakesinn.com
Abigayle's Guesthouse - 613-269-2658
The Baldachin Inn 613-269-4223
www.baldachin.com/
Lions Park Campground -
613-269-3702
Rothwell's Cottages - 613-269-3631
Riverside Campground
613-269-4664
The Avery's Guest House -
613-269-2767
Goose Island Bed & Breakfast -
613-269-4506
Gypsy Cove Bed & Breakfast -
613-269-4413
Millisle Bed & Breakfast -
613-269-3627
Rideau Bank Bed & Breakfast -
613-269-3864
Seven Gables - 613-269-2545

Kemptville

Rideau River Provincial Park -
613-258-2740
Sandy Mountain Campsite & Golf Course -
613-989-2058
Horse and Rider Bed & Breakfast -
613-258-7899

Coachhouse Restaurant and Motel - 613-258-5939

Oxford on Rideau Motel - 613-258-6275

Manotick

Water's Edge B&B, just steps from the Rideau River - 613-692-0564
www.mountainberry.biz

Brownlee House - 613-826-2201

Chilvers Bed & Breakfast - 613-692-3731

Long Island Bed & Breakfast - 613-692-2042

Olde Virginia Manor Bed & Breakfast - 613-692-4329

Ottawa

Westin Ottawa - 613-560-7000

Travelodge Hotel - 613-236-1133

The Chateau Laurier - 1-800-441-1414

Sheraton Ottawa Hotel - 1-800-489-8333

Residence Inn by Marriott - 613-231-2020

Ottawa International Hostel - 613-235-2595

Ramada Hotel & Suites - 1-800-267-8378

Quality Hotel - 1-800-228-5151

Place Minto Suites Hotel - 1-800-267-3377

Monterey Inn - 1-800-565-1311

Market Square Inn - 1-800-341-2210

Les Suites Hotel - 1-800-267-1989

Howard Johnson Plaza Hotel - 613-238-2888/1-800-446-4656

Doral Inn - 1-800-263-6725

Delta Ottawa Hotel & Suites 613-238-6000

Days Inn Ottawa - 1-800-329-7466

Carleton University Tour & Conference Centre - 613-520-5611

Albert at Bay Suites Hotel-1-800-267-6644

B&Bs Ottawa

A Mid-Towne Heritage B&B 613-236-1169

A Voyageur's Guest House 613-238-6445

Alanbury House - 613-234-8378

Alexander House - 613-789-6520

Antique Alley B&B -613-730-9667

Albert House Inn - 613-236-4479

Auberge Des Arts B&B -613-562-0909

Auberge King Edward B&B 613-565-6700

Auberge McGEE's Inn (Est. 1984) - 613-237-6089/1-800-2MCGEES

Australis Guest House - 613-235-8461

Bella Notte B&B 613-565-0497

Benner's B&B - 613-789-8320

Blue Spruces B&B - 613-236-8521

Bolton B&B 613-789-8839

Brighton House B&B- 613-233-7777

By the Way -613-232-6840

Canal View B&B - 613-234-7569

Carmichael Inn & Spa - 613-236-4667

Echo Bank House 613-730-0254

Gausthaus Switzerland B&B - 613-237-0335

Lampman House - 613-241-3696

Lyon Guest House 613-236-3904

Natural Choice/4Nature - 613-563-4399

Ottawa B&B 613-563-4399

Paterson House 613-565-8996

The Olde Bytown B&B - 613-565-7939

Hotel Kenney, Jones Falls

MAY

Navigation Season Begins on Rideau Canal - May 18, 2005 May 17, 2006 1-800-230-0016	**Victoria Day** - Holiday Monday - 3rd Monday in May	**Ottawa** **Canadian Tulip Festival** May Weeks of tulips, shows, activities... 1-800-66TULIP www.tulipfestival.ca
	**Ottawa** **Tulip Festival Flotilla** on Dows Lake and the Rideau Canal May 20, 2005 May 21, 2006 www.tulipfestival.ca	**Ottawa** **National Capital Airshow-** last weekend in May www.ottawa.com

JUNE

Kingston **Fanfayre Arts & Crafts Sale** 1-888-855-4555 www.kingstoncanada.com	**Westport** **Antique Show & Sale** 1st weekend in June 613-273-2929 www.westportrideaulakes.on.ca (613) 273-2038 or (613) 273-5451	
Portland **Portland Days** 1-877-774-3328 www.westportrideaulakes.on.ca	**Manotick** **Dickinson Days** - early June www.manotick.org	**Ottawa** **International Children's Festival, Fringe Festival, Carnival of Cultures & more** www.ottawafestivals.ca (613) 233-1085

JULY

July 1 **Canada Day** Activities and fireworks in every community. Ottawa, the nation's capital offers huge celebrations.	July 8th - 10th, 2005 **ONTARIO FAMILY FISHING WEEKEND** Fish license-free on any lake or river in Ontario. Call 1-800-667-1940. www.familyfishingweekend.com	**Kingston** **Buskers Rendezvous** 1-888-855-4555 www.kingstoncanada.com
Elgin **Elgin Days** 613-359-5108 www.westportrideaulakes.on.ca **Chaffey's Lock** **Annual Craft Market** Opinicon Lawn	**Westport** 613-273-2929 www.westportrideaulakes.on.ca	**Perth** **Perth Antique Show** early July 613-283-5270 **STEWART PARK FESTIVAL** late July-Music festival over 30 live concerts. (613) 264-1190 www.stewartparkfestival.com
Smiths Falls **Chocolate & Railroad Festival** Smiths Falls Railway Museum 1-800-257-1334 www.town.smithsfalls.on.ca	**Manotick** http://manotick.ncf.ca/index.html	**Merrickville** **Canalfest** a celebration of Merrickville's heritage & the Rideau Canal. (613) 269-4683 www.merrickville.com/chamber/
Delta **Delta Fair** Since 1830- Last weekend of July (613)928-2800 www.ruralleeds.on.ca	**Kars** **Kars Fair** third week In July host to an internationally accredited dog show 613-489-2552, or 613-692-5257 www.kars.ca	**Ottawa** **Bluesfest** 1st 2 weeks 1-866-258-3748 www.ottawa-bluesfest.ca **Jazz Festival** two weeks 613-241-2633 www.ottawajazzfestival.com

AUGUST

August 1 - Civic Holiday 'Colonel By Day' Rideau Corridor	**Kingston** **Limestone City Bluesfest** 1-888-855-4555 www.kingstoncanada.com **C.O.R.K.** Canadian Olympic Regatta Kingston 1-888-855-4555 www.kingstoncanada.com	
Portland Sun, Sand, Wind and Water Fair Third weekend of August 1-877-774-3328 www.westportrideaulakes.on.ca	**Westport** Rideau Valley Art Festival Third weekend of August **Westcraft Artisan Show** 613-273-2929 www.westportrideaulakes.on.ca	**Perth** Garlic Festival food, demonstrations, music, entertainment & more 1-877-268-BUDD 613-267-3200 www.perthgarlicfestival.com
Smiths Falls 1-800-257-1334 www.town.smiths-falls.on.ca	**Merrickville** Jewel of the Rideau Antique & Collectible Show 125 Antique dealers 613-269-2229 **1-800-934-1337**	**Ottawa** Colonel By Day Bytown Museum - (613) 234-4570 www.bytownmuseum.com Canadian Central Exhibition 613-237-7222 www.the-ex.com
Manotick-2005 30th Annual Ottawa Intl. Antique and Classic Boat Show, www.manotickclassicboatclub.ca	2006 31st Annual Ottawa International Antique and Classic Boat Show location to be announced www.manotickclassicboatclub.ca	**Gananoque** Festival of the Islands 10 day extravaganza featuring waterfront concerts, midway, boat shows, fireworks and more. 613-382-1562 or www.festivaloftheislands.com

SEPTEMBER

Labour Day Monday	Kingston	Perth
	DragonBoat Festival mid-Sept. 1-888-855-4555 www.kingstoncanada.com **Celtic Festival** mid-Sept 1-888-855-4555 www.kingstoncanada.com	**Perth Fair** Labour Day weekend 613-267-4104 Events/midway all week- end at the Fairgrounds (613) 267-4104 www.heritageperth.ca
Merrickville **Artists Studio Tour** 613-269-2229 www.merrickville.com/cha mber/	**Ottawa/Gatineau** **Gatineau Hot Air** **Balloon Festival** Canada's Largest Balloon Festival Labour Day Weekend 819-243-2331 www.balloongatineau.com	**Ottawa** 1-800-465-1867 www.ottawa.com

OCTOBER

Kingston	Chaffey's Lock	Westport
1-888-855-4555 www.kingstoncanada.com	**Studio Tour**	613-273-2929 www.westportrideaulakes. on.ca
Perth **Autumn Studio Tour** Thanksgiving Weekend 613-267-5237 or perthstudiotour.com for detailed description of the tour.	**Ottawa** 1-800-465-1867 www.ottawa.com	**Canadian** **Thanksgiving** **Weekend** **Navigation Season** **Ends** mid-October 1-800-230-0016

Cruising Guide

Ontario Waterway Cruises' Kawartha Voyageur

Boat Cruises: *Kawartha Voyageur*

Boat Rentals & Sales

The Rideau Canal at a Glance:

A Seven Day Cruising Guide

Marina Listings & Maps * Boater's Handbook

The Kawartha Voyageur

Want to explore the historic Rideau Canal but don't own a boat? No problem. There are a number of easy ways to cruise the Rideau and experience all the sights and history this system has to offer. If you don't fancy being the captain of your own vessel then consider taking a five-day voyage of adventure aboard the *Kawartha Voyageur*. It's the only live aboard riverboat plying the Rideau route between Kingston and Ottawa. These are one way trips with motor coach returns.

This floating mini-hotel with accommodations for 45 passengers, pampers guests in casual comfort as it glides along at a leisurely pace ensuring nothing is missed. This double decker ship, hand crafted by the Ackert family owners, is just a marvel of engineering and ingenuity. Over the years the demand for this type of heritage canal cruising has grown so popular the operators had to come up with some unique expansion plans for the *Kawartha Voyageur* without sacrificing the family style hospitality offered to each cruising guest. This little ship has been lengthened twice, has a retractable wheelhouse, drop-down topdeck sunroof and a bow that folds up. All these changes have produced a one of a kind vessel that fits under Rideau bridges and can squeeze in to 90-foot locks although it is 120 feet long. That's where the hinged bow comes in.

Kawartha Voyageur, locking through, bow up

photo credit: Lynda Hammond

On board guests are treated to comfortable compact sleeping cabins offering twin lower berths, toilet, sink and screened window. Showers are down the hall. There's even a cabin set up for any guest with limited mobility. Sleeping quarters are at water level and the second deck accommodates the dining room and lounge. Windows all around offer guests a panoramic view all of the time. An elevator links the cabin and dining/lounge level. And there's more. The top sun deck offers spectacular views and if the sun's too hot there is plenty of seating under the huge canopy. For those wanting more of a feel for the water the forward and aft decks offer shaded vantage viewing spots.

The *Kawartha Voyageur* offers all the comforts of home too. Quiet generators provide electricity for heating, central air conditioning and lighting. But that's the technical stuff. How about the food? The Ackerts actually come from a farming background and all the meals on board are wholesome, home-cooked and delicious. What's also great about cruising the Rideau on the *Kawartha Voyageur* is that it stops each night of the trip at a historic town or lock station for more exploring, shopping and dockside fun. And the onboard digital piano/organ isn't just for show. Captain Marc Ackert, other family members and the crew lead some mighty nostalgic singalongs in the evening while enroute.

The *Kawartha Voyageur* has a busy sailing schedule offering both trips on the Rideau Canal and Trent-Severn Waterway from early spring until mid-October. To find out more about cruising opportunities contact **Ontario Waterway Cruises** at 1-800-561-5767 or write to OWC Box 6 Orillia, Ontario, L3V 6H9 www.ontariowaterwaycruises.com

Cruises

Whatever type of cruise you are interested in you'll find it on the Rideau.

Gananoque Boat Line 3 hour and 1 hour tours - 613-382-2146

Classic Paddle Wheel Riverboat, Kingston-1000 Islands Cruise Line

Kingston-1000 Islands Cruises - 1-800-848-0011 or 613-549-5544 - 1.5 to 3 hour tours of 1000 Islands Reservations are recommended. www.1000islandscruises.on.ca

St. Lawrence Cruise Lines- 1-800-267-7868 - offers river cruise vacations, cruising the St. Lawrence and Ottawa Rivers. www.stlawrence-cruiselines.com

The Harriet By, (Merrickville) electric launch. Glide quietly along the beautiful Rideau Waterway enjoying a 45 minute journey that takes you through the Rideau Bird Sanctuary to the Osprey nest and then returns to *The Depot* along the original channel of the Rideau River. Trips run between 11 am and 5 pm daily and can accommodate up to seven passengers per trip. You can book a tour by visiting *The Depot*, or if you wish to make a reserva-

tion in advance you can call *The Depot* at 613-269-9333. Visit www.rideaufriends.com for more information.

Paul's Boat Lines Ltd. - 613-225-6781 - cruises along the Rideau Canal in the heart of the Ottawa.

Rideau Canal Boat Tours
Classic Rideau Cruises

Cruise the most unique section of the historic Rideau Canal with live commentary on its history.
Daily tours from Chaffey's Lock to Jones Falls and back. Departing 9:00a.m. and 2:00p.m. Also offering an overnight package that includes dinner at *The Galley* in Portland, accommodation at *Portland Bay Bed and Breakfast*, morning boat cruise/tour and lunch at *The Opinicon* at Chaffey's Lock.
Other packages include:
Lunch package 1: Morning cruise and lunch at *The Opinicon*
Lunch package 2: Lunch at *The Opinicon* and afternoon cruise at 2:00p.m.
Dinner Package: Afternoon cruise and dinner at *The Opinicon*
For more information visit the website: www.rideauboattours.com or www.bbcanada.com/portlandbay or write to: Portland Bay Bed & Breakfast - 22 Water St. Portland, ON, K0G 1V0
Tel:613-272-0222 email:boattour@istar.ca

Captain and tour guide, Lance Jervis-Read of Rideau Canal Boat Tours dressed in a replica English Naval Captain's uniform. His vessel "Chuckles", originally built in 1940 and restored from 1986-1994, is seen here docked at Chaffey's Lock..

Houseboats & more...

$\mathcal{F}$or waterway explorers wanting to pilot their own little ships for an adventure vacation or a day of sight seeing there are a number of other options available. Houseboating has long been a great way to meander through the Rideau.

There are a few main pontoon style houseboat companies, *Waterway Get-A-Way Houseboat Vacations* and *Rideau Lakes Houseboats*, serving the Rideau with vessels up to 40 feet long cruising out of Smiths Falls and Portland respectively. *Fun-a-Float* boat rentals in Portland also rents houseboats as well as other vessels.

These locations are advantageous because renters have the benefit of being in the centre of the system. They can plan a vacation that allows for several cruising options - staying in the main larger Rideau Lakes area, heading towards Ottawa or south towards Kingston and back.

Going in any direction still spells an extraordinary holiday opportunity. Houseboats offer all the comforts of home with sleeping accommodations that range between six and ten adults. Ideal for families or small groups.

For those wanting to operate a real cabin cruiser, *Aylings Boatyard* in Merrickville operates *Bare Boat Charters* - steel built mid-size rental boats. The cruisers range from 27 to 30 feet and sleep up to 6 people. Call 613-269-4969 or 1-888-818-3140 for information.

Another emerging style of chartering exists with the availability of open deck outboard motor powered pontoon boats that can be rented from a number of marinas along the waterway. These versatile 18-22 foot boats have tons of room, comfortable seating, ample storage and are very easy to operate especially for those with limited boating experience.

With these boats, waterway visitors can take day, weekend, or week long trips from various locations. Also, the option exists to go **"cruise camping"** exploring by day and tenting overnight at different lockstations or perhaps doing a **"cruise inn"** tour where it's boating by day and stopping overnight to enjoy a comfy room ashore at any number of bed and breakfast homes and country inns that are positioned in the welcoming towns and villages that dot the Rideau Canal corridor.

Boat Rentals & Sales

Kingston - Ahoy Rentals - 613-539-3202 - Located on Kingston's waterfront, rentals for day sailing, canoeing, sea kayaking, 24', 26'&33' sailboat for bare boat charters.www.ahoyrentals.com

Seeley's Bay - *Melody Lodge & Marina* - 613-387-3497 - Boat & motor rentals, canoes and paddle boats.

Chaffey's Lock - *Brown's Marina* - 613-359-5466 - Offers boats & motors for sale including pontoon deck boats and fishing boats, and more powered by Evinrude and Johnson. Showroom in Crosby on Hwy 15- 613-272-5466.www.brownsmarina.com

Newboro - Clear Lake Cottages - 613-272-2745- Offers 19' pontoon fishing boats, 14' fiberglass boats - daily or weekly rentals available.

Stirling Lodge offers several fishing boats for rent from 14' to 20'- 613-272-2435 or www.stirlinglodge.com

Portland- *Len's Cove Marina* - 613-272-2581 - Offers variety of rentals from 14' fishing boats to 20' pontoon boats. New and Used boat sales. Mercury Platinum Dealer.

Fun-a-Float Boat Rentals - Offers fishing boats, skiing boats, jet boats, bowriders, pontoon boats and houseboats. Call 613-272-2835 or visit their website www.fun-a-float.com

Rideau Lakes Houseboats (sleep up to 10), located on Big Rideau Lake. P.O. Box 239, Portland, Ontario, K0G 1V0. 1-800-775-6663, or 613-272-5089 www.rideauhouseboats.com

Merrickville - Aylings Boatyard Bare Boat Charters- 613-269-4969/1-888-818-3140 - Offers cruiser charters. 3 cruisers 27 to 30 ft. sleep up to 6 people.

Canadian Recreational Canoe Association - 613-269-2910 or 1-888-252-6292 rents canoes and kayaks. Courses & tours available.

Manotick - *Hurst Marina* - 613-692-1234 - offers large variety of boats for sale or rent. Including Searay, Baja, Boston Whaler, Legend Boats, Mercury. www.hurstmarina.com

Rideau Canal At A Glance

Much of Ontario's most beautiful scenery and delightful villages are found along its inland waterways. The Rideau is a perfect example of this. Steeped in history, this 202 km (125 mile) stretch of lakes, rivers and man made canals forge the inland link between Ottawa and Kingston.

The following boating itinerary is based on a seven day plan, although the timetable can vary depending on special interests and waterway traffic. A traveller may find it more expedient to arrange lock-through times during the week to avoid weekend traffic and to coordinate stops at canal corridor towns with local fairs and festivals.

We recommend that the boater, to allow ample time for sight-seeing and exploring, consider six to seven days for this one way trip. If transporting a boat by trailer, consider this option: Launch the boat in Kingston and make the trip to Ottawa where a bus can be easily taken back to the car and trailer. The trip to Ottawa by car is two hours. This option is for those who have a limited timetable, the return trip by boat is three to four days.

The Rideau is easily navigated. Built as a 'slackwater' system, there are no excessive currents in the rivers. Each lock has plenty of canal staff ready and able to help novice boaters locking through.
The Rideau Canal is well marked with buoys. It is important to note that when the watershed at Newboro is reached the red and green buoys will be reversed. Enjoy the trip!

Boats on Big Rideau Lake

Cruising Big Rideau Lake

Photo Credit: Steve Weir, Rideau Canal, Parks Canada

Day One

*I*n Kingston the boater finds two excellent docking facilities: **Portsmouth Olympic Harbour** and **Confederation Basin Marina**. The latter is located in the heart of old **Kingston** across from City Hall. A tourist information centre can be found opposite the marina. It is here that one can obtain directions to Fort Henry, the Marine Museum and a multitude of other wonderful places to visit. Behind City Hall is the site of an open air market. The city itself is well worth exploring to see the many old limestone buildings and to visit the plenitude of antique shops, boutiques and restaurants.

To begin the journey in Kingston, charts 1513-5 will be needed. Locking-through at Kingston Mills in the morning will increase the chances of reaching Jones Falls by night. It is no longer necessary for U.S. visitors to stop in Kingston for Customs Clearance. A direct line to Canada Customs is available at Kingston Mills.

Once under the bridge at Highway 2, cosmopolitan boating is left behind. The terrain along the Cataraqui River is low and grassy. When approaching Kingston Mills locks, the landscape changes drastically. The river narrows and the grasslands give way to steep granite cliffs. There are four locks here with a total lift of 45 feet to Colonel By Lake. A short stop at the upstream lock will allow for a visit to the Blockhouse Museum and Anglin Centre, the original lockmaster's house. This blockhouse is one of four along the Rideau which were originally built to defend strategic locations against canal attack.

Continuing upstream through Colonel By Lake and the River Styx is Lower Brewers Lock or Washburn. The swing bridge at Lower Brewers Lock has a clearance of 4 to 5 feet, depending on water levels. Once through, a short jog upstream will bring you to the two locks at Upper Brewers. You may decide to dock at Upper Brewers Lock for the night and not proceed to Jones Falls. Another option would be to continue through to Cranberry Lake and Little Cranberry Lake to Seeley's Bay. Here you will find groceries, beer and liquor stores, restaurants and a motel. **Melody Lodge & Marina** is located SW of marker 222 and offers full marina service.

From Seeley's Bay it is roughly 5 miles/7.5 km through Whitefish Lake to Jones Falls. About midway is Morton Bay. Anchorage here is popular with boaters because of its scenic location amidst high, wooded cliffs. The next stop is Jones Falls which has one of the highest dams of its kind in North America and the third highest such dam in the world. It takes about an hour and a half to pass through the four locks which have a combined lift of approximately 60 feet. The lockmaster's house is open to the public and the Blacksmith shop is definitely worth a visit. Stop here for a meal or accommodation at **Hotel Kenney**, docking facilities are also available.

Day Two

From Jones Falls it is approximately 6 miles/10 km to Chaffey's Lock. This community has been a popular vacation spot for over a century. There are several marinas and lodges in the vicinity as well as groceries, a post office and laundromat. There is ample tie up space at Chaffey's. A restored defensible lockmaster's house, which was built in 1844, is now the Lockmaster's House Museum operated by the Chaffey's Lock and Area Heritage Society. A stop here for lunch at the **Opinicon Resort** is recommended and a stroll up the road to **Cedars Art Studio** for some delightful shopping. If you choose to spend more time here docking and full marine service is available at **Brown's Marina**. The Opinicon also offers docking if you choose to stay over.

Upon leaving Chaffey's Lock proceed through Indian Lake, Clear Lake and Newboro Lake to Newboro. This village proves a lovely visit with ample tie-up space at the lock and at the public dock in the village, close to all amenities. At least take time to do some shopping, at Kilborn's-on-the-Rideau or Loon Village. Because Newboro is the summit of the Rideau, keep in mind that the red and green buoys will be reversed as you leave the lock.

Once into Upper Rideau Lake the route west into Westport is recommended. Located at the north-west side of the lake, the village of Westport makes for a charming overnight stay. The harbour provides docking facilities. A foot bridge leads to a parkette on shore where it is only a half block to the main shopping area. Westport boasts many shops, restaurants and a waterside inn offers luxury accommodation and dining. There are beer and liquor stores, a laundromat, bank machine and post office and over 100 shops. The Rideau District Museum on Bedford street was originally a blacksmith shop and is very interesting to visit.

Day Three

When departing from Westport, head back to the main channel and proceed through the Narrows Lock. Although there are no supplies available at this lock, it is worth visiting the blockhouse which was built in 1833 and restored in 1960. Due to often gusty winds here, it is best to tie up downstream where it is more sheltered.

The clear waters of Big Rideau Lake have been a source of pleasure to boaters and anglers for over a century. On the south-east side of the lake lies Portland, which is a great port for overnight docking at **Len's Cove Marina** and a bite to eat at **The Galley Restaurant**. Portland has a beautiful waterfront and attracts many vacationers with its excellent swimming and fishing. There are several marinas in town and the large public wharf is close to restaurants, groceries, beer and liquor stores and accommodations

Day Four

Head back to the main channel upon leaving Portland. Then it is on to Murphys Point Provincial Park where there are wilderness docking facilities for the convenience of campers. Information is available at the park office in Nobles Bay. As well as having some wonderful hiking trails, which are steeped in local history and a mine to explore, the park offers four boat-in camping areas.

Rideau Ferry is the next port enroute and has marina facilities, the Shipwreck Restaurant and a public wharf. A fuel up here is recommended because there are no gas docks or pump-out facilities between here and Merrickville.

About two miles past Rideau Ferry is the entrance to the Tay Canal. This spur route passes through Upper and Lower Beveridges Locks and continues to the beautiful town of Perth, well worth a visit.

The main channel, however, proceeds through Lower Rideau Lake to Poonamalie Lock. From this picturesque locksite it is just over two miles to Smiths Falls Detached Lock. There is abundant tie-up space at this lock which is about a fifteen minute walk from downtown. In the heart of downtown near the hydraulic lock is **Victoria Park** which has excellent docking facilities including hydro, water, showers, and pump-out. There is also a playground and wading pool for children. **Smiths Falls** has a variety of restaurants, shops, and services for visitors. Don't forget to visit the Rideau Canal Museum located at 34 Beckwith Street South.

Day Five

*L*ess than one mile downstream from the hydraulic lock is Old Sly's Locks. These locks are located about a 1/2 mile walk to **Hershey's Chocolate Shoppe® Visitors Centre** where factory tours occur daily. Close to the lower lock is Lower Reach Park which has docking facilities, tennis courts and a picnic area. Just east of the park is Heritage House Museum.

The next two locks are Edmunds and Kilmarnock. Both are secluded and quiet. Kilmarnock is a bird-watcher's paradise. From here it is about 20 kms/10 miles to Merrickville. This historic village is definitely worth visiting. Plenty of tie-up space is available upstream of the locks which are right in the heart of the village.This ideal place holds many fine old homes, cafés, restaurants, antique shops, boutiques, groceries, beer and liquor stores, as well as fine accommodations. Sam Jakes Inn and The Baldachin Inn offer fine dining, luxury accommodation. You can dock at the wharf in 'the pond' or at Aylings Marina. Stop in at the Friends of the Rideau's retail outlet **'The Depot'** for souvenirs and Rideau information. The **Canadian Recreational Canoeing Association** Headquarters are also located here. A visit to the Industrial Heritage Complex is very interesting and a shopping trip at **Mirick's Landing** for some unique items is definitely in order. Drop in at the **Round the Corner Bakeshop** for fresh pastries, and picnic treats.

Day Six

*A*pproximately two miles downstream from Merrickville is Clowes Lock and Nicholson's Lock. Many of the older homes along this stretch of the river face the water. This is because this river was the main mode of transport in the early years. Almost four miles further along is Burritts Rapids where there is tie-up space at the floating docks in the river channel. **Michael's Restaurant** and a coin laundry can be found just steps from Burritts Rapids Lock.

The cruise from Burritts Rapids to Long Island is beautiful. Known as the Long Reach, it is the longest lock-free stretch on the system and is very tranquil offering lots to see and do. A quick trip up Kemptville Creek is also in order for small draught boats. Tie up is available at the Kemptville town dock.

Your next stop is Manotick. Stay at **Manotick Marina** and visit nearby **Miller's Berry Farm**. Quaint shops, all amenities and good food can be found in this lovely village. Of historical interest is Watson's Mill, part of the Dickinson Square Conservation Area. The night can be spent at **Manotick Marina** or the Long Island Locks, about one mile downstream, which provides ample tie-up space or at **Hurst Marina**, a fully licensed restaurant **The Swan on the Rideau** is located on site. Another option is to continue on and dock at **Dows Lake Pavilion,** home of **Malone's Restaurant** in Ottawa. This lake and marina facility is approximately 11 miles/18 km downstream from Long Island Locks.

7 Day Seven

Approximately 5 miles from Long Island is Black Rapids Lock. This is the last "rural" lock before Ottawa. Time permitting, pause at Hogs Back Lock. An interpretive trail, one mile in length, runs from the lock station to the dam. If time allows, take advantage of the great beach at Mooney's Bay. Hartwells Locks are part of the man-made canal which begins at the flight locks in Ottawa. This quiet lockstation is surrounded by beautiful parklands and the Arboretum, Experimental Farm and botanical garden which is all open to the public. About a mile downstream is **Dows Lake Pavilion** which has marina services and a variety of restaurants including **Malone's Lakeside Bar & Grill**. There is also a boat ramp here which you may want to keep in mind for your car and trailer.

The final leg of the journey is a very cosmopolitan one, despite the greenspace that borders the canal. If you are not planning to lock through the flight locks to the Ottawa River you can tie-up upstream and explore the city. Enjoy the shops and sights of the **ByWard Market** and dine at **The Fish Market Restaurant**. At the Flight Locks is the Bytown Museum, definitely worth a visit to learn a lot about canal history. If you do continue your excursion down the flight locks and onto the Ottawa River, docking, marina facilities and dining can be found at the **Rockcliffe Boathouse**.

Where to Dock

𝒯he maps should be used to locate marinas, public wharfs, locks and towns. The following pages describe the facilities and services that are available at the marinas.

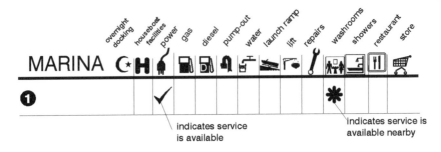

The above chart displays the services provided by each marina. A check below the graphic will indicate that the particular service can be found. The number beside the marina name and address indicates the location on the corresponding map. Navigational draught is 5 feet throughout the system and may be shallower at docks. We recommend contacting the marinas for further information and reservations.

Every effort has been made to ensure that the data in this book is accurate. However, changing conditions make it impossible to guarantee one hundred percent accuracy. Thank you to Parks Canada for allowing us to use their map of the Rideau Canal.

Boaters cruising the Rideau Canal must purchase hydrographic charts 1512 and 1513. These can be obtained by contacting the Friends of the Rideau at 1 Jasper Ave. Smiths Falls, Ontario, K7A 4B5 or call 613-283-5810 www.rideaufriends.com.

See page 7 of this guide for a list of chart dealers and other information sources.

Confederation Basin
Kingston

Refer to Chart 1513-5 - Washburn to Kingston

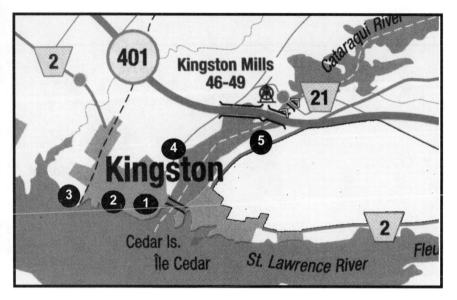

MARINA	☪★	H	🔌	⛽	🚿	⚓	🚰	🛥	🪝	🔧	🚻	🛏	🍽	🛒
1 Confederation Basin Marina *Kingston* 613-546-4291	✓	✓	✓			✓	✓	✓	✓	✓	✓	✓		❋
2 Portsmouth Olympic Harbour *Kingston* 613-546-4291	✓	✓	✓	✓	✓	✓	✓	✓			✓	✓	❋	✓
3 Collins Bay Marina *Kingston* 613-389-4455 www.collinsbaymarina.com	✓		✓	✓	✓	✓		✓		✓	✓	❋	❋	
4 Kingston Marina 613-549-7747	✓	✓	✓	✓	✓	✓	✓	✓	✓		✓	✓	❋	❋
5 Rideau Marina *Kingston* 1-888-407-1784	✓	✓	✓	✓		✓	✓	✓	✓	✓	✓	✓	❋	❋

★ To make reservations at either **Flora McDonald Confederation Basin** located in the heart of downtown Kingston or **Portsmouth Olympic Harbour** call 613-546-4291 or visit www.city.kingston.on.ca for more information.

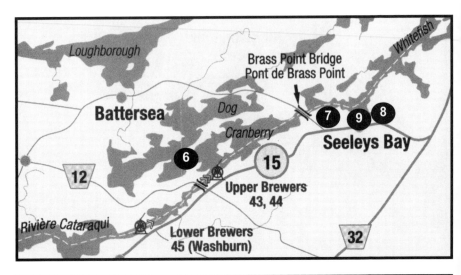

MARINA	☾	H	⛽	⛽	⛽	⚓	🚰	🔩	🏗	🔧	🚻	🛏	🍴	🛒
6 MelodyLodge &Marina *Cranberry Lake* 613-387-3497 www.melodylodge.ca	✓	✓	✓	✓	✓	✓	✓	✓			✓	✓		✓
7 Rideau Breeze Marina *Seeley's Bay* 613-387-3100				✓		✓					✓			✓
8 Seeley's Bay Public Dock 613-659-3080	✓	✓	✓				✓				❋	❋	❋	❋
9 Sunny Acres Resort & Marina *Seeley's Bay* 613-387-3379				✓			✓							

★ **Melody Lodge and Marina**, located just south west of Marker 222 offers full service Marina facilities including diesel and gas, pumpout, overnight docking, 15 and 30 amp power, bbqs and picnic area, public phone and datajack for laptop downloading, fishing licenses, tackle and more. Call for reservations and information: 1-888-MELODY-1 or 613-387-3497 or visit www.melodylodge.ca

Refer to Chart 1513-4 - Jones Falls to Washburn

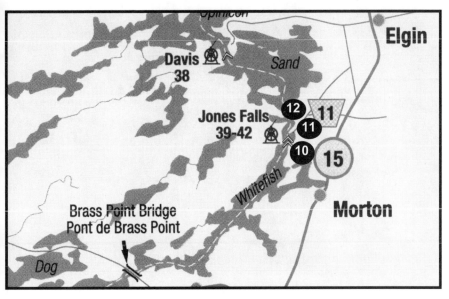

MARINA	☾★	H	⚡	🅱 🅳	⚓	💧	✂	🏗	🔧	👪	🛏	🍴	🛒
⑩ Hotel Kenney Jones Falls 613-359-5500 www.hotelkenney.com	✓	✓	✓	✓		✓	✓	✓		✓		✓	✓
⑪ Shangri-la Marina & Lodge Jones Falls 613-359-5774	✓		✓	✓		✓	✓	✓	✳	✓	✓	✓	✓
⑫ Sand Lake Marine 1 mi. north of Jones Falls 613-359-5612			✓			✓	✓						

★ **Hotel Kenney** offers boaters overnight dockage, shore power, gas dock with pump out, a coin laundry, grocery store and snack bar. Call 613-359-5500 or 1-866-KENNEYS or visit www.hotelkenney.com

Hotel Kenney - Jones Falls

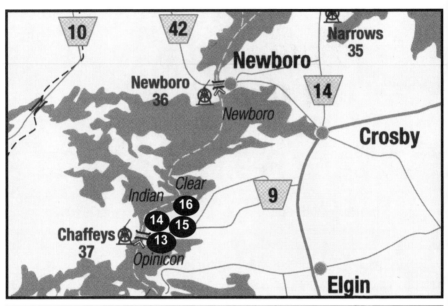

MARINA	☾	H	🔌	⛽	🅳	🍶	🚰	🛏	🧹	🔧	🚻	🛗	🍴	🛒
⑬ Opinicon Resort Marina *Chaffey's Lock* 613-359-5233	✓	✓	✓	✓		✓	✓				✓	✓	✓	✓
⑭ Brown's Marina *Chaffey's Lock* 613-359-5466 www.brownsmarina.com	✓	✓	✓	✓		✓	✓	✓	✓	✓			✿	✿
⑮ Franklin's Marina *Chaffey's Lock* 613-359-5457	✓		✓			✓	✓		✓	✓			✿	✿

★ **The Opinicon Resort Hotel** has 700 feet of docks below Chaffey's Locks, showers, washrooms, grocery store, fuel, ice, gift shop, coffee bar and more. Call 613-359-5233 for reservations, www.theopiniconresorthotel.com

★ **Brown's Marina** offers full sales and service facilities, 200 feet of gas dock, w/water, hydro and pumpout, marine store, overnight dockage, and qualified mechanics on duty 7 days a week. Call 613-359-5466 or visit www.brownsmarina.com.

Refer to Chart 1513-3 – Newboro to Jones Falls & 1513-2 – Rocky Narrows to Newboro

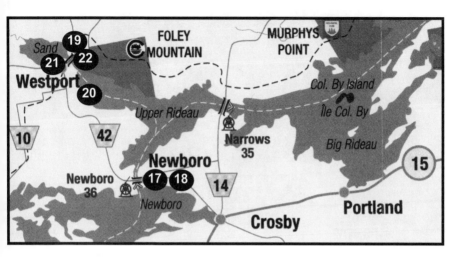

MARINA	☾★	H	⚡	⛽	🛢	⚓	🚿	🛥	⛴	🔧	🚻	🛏	🍴	🛒
16 Indian Lake Marina 613-359-5779	✓	✓	✓	✓		✓	✓	✓	✳	✓	✓	✓		✳
17 Newboro Public Wharf	✓	✓											✳	✳
18 Stirling Lodge *Newboro* 613-272-2435				✓										
19 The Cove Country Inn *Westport* 613-273-3636 www.coveinn.com	✓	✓	✓				✓	✓			✓		✓	✳
20 Westport Municipal Harbour	✓	✓	✓	✳		✳	✓	✳		✳	✓		✳	✳
21 Graham's Marine *Westport* 613-273-2882										✓				✳
22 Manser's Marina *Westport* 613-273-2797				✓		✓		✳			✳	✳	✳	✳

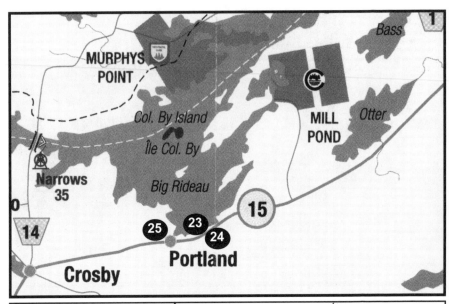

MARINA	☾	H	⛽	⛽	⛽	⚓	🚰	🛶	🏗	🔧	🚻	🛏	🍴	🛒
Portland Public Wharf ㉓ *Portland*	✓	✓	✓				✓				※	※	※	※
BayviewYacht Harbour *Portland* ㉔ 613-272-2787 www.bayviewyachtharbour.com	✓	✓	✓	✓		✓	✓	✓	✓	✓	✓	✓	※	※
Len's Cove Marina ㉕ *Portland* 613-272-2581 www.lenscove.com	✓	✓	✓	✓	✓	✓	✓	✓	✓	✓	✓	✓	✓	※

★ **Len's Cove Marina** offers guest dockage, gas & diesel, pump out, parts and service, 25 ton lift, showers/washrooms, boat rentals, pool and laundry. Call 613-272-2581 or visit www.lenscove.com. On site enjoy the fun relaxing atmosphere and great food at **The Galley Restaurant**.

Refer to Chart 1513-1-Smiths Falls to Rocky Narrows

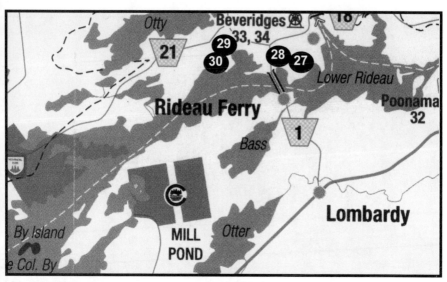

MARINA	☪	H	⬗	⛽	🛢	⚓	🚰	🛶	🚤	🔧	🚻	🛏	🍴	🛒
27 Rideau Ferry Public Wharf	✓	✓											✽	✽
28 The Shipwreck 613-264-0812	✓	✓								✓		✓	✓	
29 Rideau Ferry Marine Ltd. 613-267-3512						✓	✓	✓	✓	✓			✽	✽
30 Rideau Ferry Harbour 613-264-2628	✓	✓	✓	✓		✓	✓	✓	✓	✓	✓	✓	✽	✽

Public Wharf at Rideau Ferry

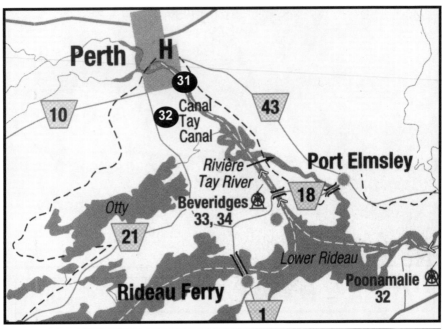

MARINA	☪★	H	🔌	⛽	🛢	🚰	🚿	🔧	⚓	🚻	🛏	🍽	🛒
31 Last Duel Park *Perth* 613-267-0214	✓	✓	✓				✓	✓	✓		❋	❋	
32 Perth Public Wharf	✓										❋	❋	

Perth Turning Basin and the Crystal Palace - Farmers Market, accessible to small craft only

Refer to Chart 1513-1 Smiths Falls to Rocky Narrows

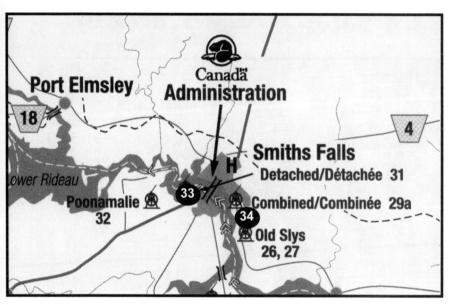

Port Elmsley

Canada **Administration**

18

4

Smiths Falls
Detached/Détachée 31

Lower Rideau

Poonamalie 32

H

Combined/Combinée 29a

Old Slys 26, 27

MARINA	C★	H	🔌	⛽	⛽	🚰	🪚	🏴	🔧	🚻	🛏	🍴	🛒
Victoria Park Marina ③③ *Smiths Falls* 613-283-5112	✓	✓	✓		✓	✓				✓	✓	❉	❉
③④ **Comfort Inn** *Smiths Falls* 613-283-5150	✓		✓							✓		❉	❉

★ **Victoria Park Marina** offers overnight docking, water, power, wading pool and play ground. Campsites are available. Contact the town of Smiths Falls for more information at 1-800-257-1334 or visit www.town.smiths-falls.on.ca

docks at Victoria park

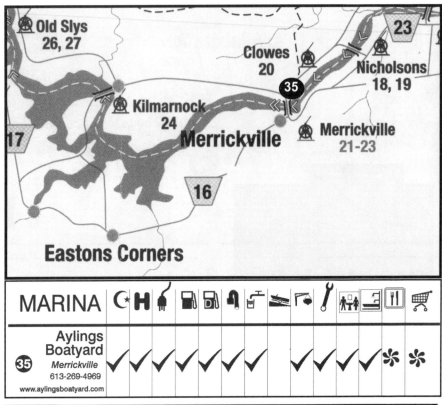

MARINA	☪	H	🔌	⛽	⛽	💧	🚿	⚓	🪝	🔧	👫	🛏	🍽	🛒
③⑤ **Aylings Boatyard** *Merrickville* 613-269-4969 www.aylingsboatyard.com	✓	✓	✓	✓	✓	✓		✓	✓	✓	✓	❇	❇	

Ottawa International Antique and Classic Boatshow at Aylings Boatyard, Merrickville

Refer to Chart 1512-2

Long Island to Becketts Landing

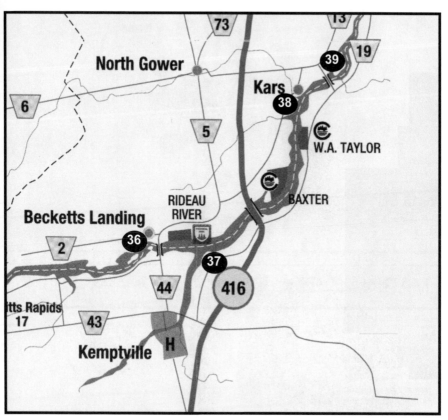

MARINA	C★	H	⚡	⛽	⛽	🔧	💧	🛶	⚓	🔧	🚻	🛏	🍽	🛒
Ludlow's Boat Works **36** *Beckett's Landing* 613-258-4270	✓		✓				✓	✓	✓	✓	✓			✓
Pirate Cove Marina **37** *Kemptville* 613-258-2325 piratecovemarina.com	✓	✓	✓	✓	✓	✓	✓	✓	✓	✓	✓	✓	❄	❄
Kars Public **Wharf** **38**	✓							✓					❄	❄
Long Island Marine **39** *Kars* 613-489-2747 longislandmarine.com	✓	✓	✓			✓	✓	✓	✓	✓	✓	✓	❄	❄

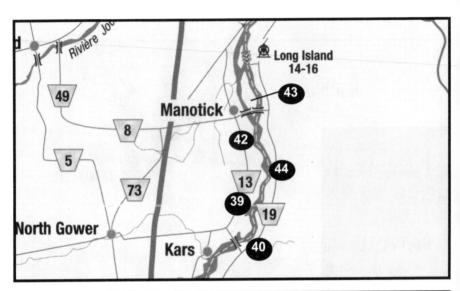

MARINA	☾	H	⚡	⛽	⛽	⚓	🚰	🛥	⛿	🔧	🚻	🧺	🍴	🛒
Long Island Marine *Kars* ㊴ 613-489-2747 www.longislandmarine.com	✓	✓	✓			✓	✓	✓	✓	✓	✓	✓	✻	✻
Hurst Marina *Manotick* ㊵ 613-692-1234 www.hurstmarina.com	✓		✓	✓	✓	✓	✓		✓	✓	✓	✓	✓	✓
Manotick Marina Inc. ㊷ 613-692-4083	✓		✓	✓		✓	✓	✓	✓	✓	✓	✓	✓	✓
Manotick Public Wharf ㊸	✓	✓					✓						✻	✻
Kelly's Landing *Manotick* ㊹				✓	✓								✓	✓

★ **Hurst Marina** has everything a boater needs. Transient dockage, power, gas, parts & service, laundry, washrooms, showers, store, pool and hot tub, as well as boat sales and rentals. A great restaurant can be found on-site. Call 613-692-1234 or www.hurstmarina.com

★ **Manotick Marina** - Full service marina with dockage - 613-692-4083- laundry, showers, playground, power, gas, pumpout & more.

Refer to Chart 1512-1
Ottawa Locks to Long Island

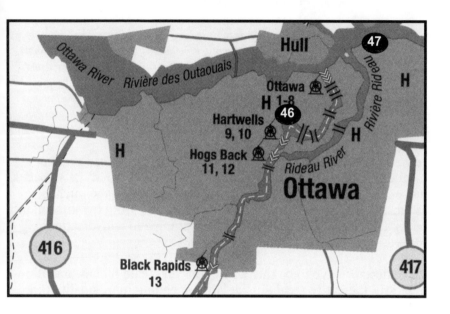

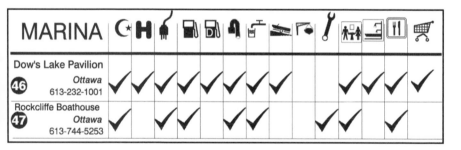

★ **Dows Lake Pavilion** offers a full service marina right in the heart of Ottawa. Call 613-232-5278 for reservations and information or visit www.dowslake.com.

★ **Rockcliffe Boathouse**, downstream from the Ottawa Flightlocks on the Ottawa River, offers docking, gas and a licensed restaurant. Call 613-744-5253 for reservations.

Summer Grilling Wines

by Shari Darling

Shari Darling is the feature food writer for the Peterborough Examiner and a syndicated food and wine pairing columnist. A newspaper journalist by trade, Shari Darling enjoys a North American reputation in food and wine. Author of 4 books, Shari is presently releasing her latest work, a cookbook entitled "Harmony On The Palate," which celebrates the new evolution in food and wine pairing through recipes and matching wine notes.

One of the enjoyable aspects of grilling is that you can entertain guests outside, on the boat or at the cottage. One of the setbacks, however, is that much of the meal is often prepared in the kitchen. This means your guests must watch as you scurry from the kitchen to the deck and back. This can make entertaining and conversations awkward.

Grilling doesn't have to be this way. You can create menus that allow you to grill the entire meal outside, thus spending more quality time with family and friends. Keep the menu simple. Focusing on seasonal ingredients, simple serving methods and as little time as possible in the house. Avoid glass plates. Napkins and foam plates are perfectly suitable. Plastic, colourful wineglasses that match the napkins add flare to the festivities.

Be fully prepared before your guests arrive. Grilling time should take no more than a half hour. Spend three to five minutes at the grill for each course. The grill is primarily used to reheat or quickly grill simple foods. Carrots, turnips, potatoes and squash can be par cooked. Asparagus, mushrooms, and zucchini can be put directly on the grill. When grilling vegetables, allow them to get soft, but remain crisp.

Seafood and shellfish should be grilled or seared quickly over high heat. Delicate fish, such as sole, can be placed in a wire grill basket. They should be seared quickly for a few minutes over high heat. Firm fish, such as salmon or shark can be placed directly on the grill. If using a marinade, marinate fish for no longer than 30 minutes in the refrigerator. If you intend to serve the marinade as a sauce, be sure to boil it for a few minutes to kill any potential bacteria from the raw fish. Shellfish, such as oysters and mussels can be placed on the hottest part of the grill until they open.

Chicken can be par cooked then finished on the grill on medium heat for a few minutes each side. Grilling raw chicken is more risky as the flesh tends to dry out. The sugar in sauces also can burn, and therefore should be used at the end of grilling.

The desired doneness for beef will determine the level of heat on the grill. Generally, beef needs higher heat for a longer period. Rare and medium rare steaks must be cooked quickly over high heat. Medium to well-done steaks should be placed on the coolest side of the grill. They need lower heat for a longer period. The best cuts for grilling are between one and a quarter to two and a quarter inches in thickness. Cuts thicker than this won't grill well. And always refrain from using salt until the end. Salt draws the moisture out of the beef. Carefully watch seafood. Shrimp and scallops, for example, need about five minutes total on the grill, two and a half minutes each side. Too many people overcook seafood and it becomes rubbery.

White wines and rosés are ideal for grilling, as both are chilled. Rosés look festive, especially the ones with a bright, salmon colour. Lemon-based or vinegar-based marinades or sauces work well with crisp, dry whites like dry Riesling, Sauvignon Blanc, Pinot Blanc and/or Pinot Grigio. Sweet based sauces – which include those with ketchup – are best to be paired to a wine with a hint of sweetness. Off-dry Riesling or an off-dry rosé is ideal. Berry sauces for chicken and ribs have sweetness from the sugar in preserves. Pair berry sauces or any fruit chutney with a wine with a hint of sweetness as well. Hot and spicy sauces also need a wine with  some sweetness. The sweetness offsets the heat and refreshes the palate. Fill a wine cooler up with ice and water and wait for your guests to arrive.

When entertaining, be prepared for overnight guests.

When entertaining, do whatever it takes to make sure your guests never drink and drive. Arrange for a designated driver, call them a cab, or offer them a place to stay overnight. For more responsible hosting tips, check out *HOST: LCBO's guide for responsible entertaining* at www.lcbo.com.

Please Drink Responsibly

General Information

Hours of Operation for 2005

May 21-June 10	Monday to Thursday	8:30am to 4:30pm
	Friday to Sunday	8:30am to 7:30pm
	Holiday Monday	8:30am to 7:30pm
June 11-Sept. 6		8:30am to 7:30pm
Sept. 7-Sept 13		8:30am to 4:30pm
Sept. 14-Oct. 13	Tuesday to Thursday	9:30am to 3:30pm
	Friday to Monday	9:30am to 4:30pm

-Times of first and last lockages of the day are not guaranteed.
-Lockage times are also affected by heavy traffic, water management and other lock-station duties
-Last Bridge Swing occurs ten minutes prior to station closure

(**Please Note**: The hours above are subject to change. We recommend contacting Parks Canada to confirm hours and rates before departure. Contact numbers and address can be found at the end of this section.)
To ensure last lockage arrive 30 minutes before closing per lock chamber at each lockstation. At Ottawa flight locks allow 3.5 hours. At swing bridges allow 10 minutes.

Bridge Schedules

Most swing/lift bridges operate on an on-demand schedule. Some areas certain restrictions apply.

Ottawa: swing/lift bridges remain closed during rush hour traffic from Monday to Friday; 8:30-9:00 am, 12:30-1:15 pm, and 3:30-5:30 pm.

Smiths Falls Bridge, from June 23 to August 6, opens at 8:45, 9:30, 10:15, 11:00, and 11:45 am. It operates on-demand after 1:00 pm.

Old Slys Bridge, remains closed during weekdays from 11:55 am to 12:15 pm and 12:45 to 1:00 pm.

Perth's Beckwith Street Bridge swings open at 11:00 am and 3:30 pm during the summer and 11:00h and 2:30 pm in the fall.

Entry fees are charged at most national parks or historic sites. The bulk of the money raised through admission fees remains for use by that particular site. Entry fees are often voluntary, look for collection boxes and invest in the sites future.

2005 Permits and Fees for Lockage and Mooring*

Type of Permit	Rates
Single Lockage and Return	$0.85/ft
One Day Lockage	$1.50/ft
Six Day	$4.60/ft
Seasonal Lockage	$8.10/ft
Transit (one way)	$4.25/ft
Overnight Mooring	$0.70/ft
Seasonal Overnight Mooring	$9.00/ft
Power**	$7.00 per night
Commercial Seasonal Lockage	$26.40/ft
Rental Houseboat Seasonal Lockage	$12.00/ft
Commercial Seasonal Overnight Mooring	$16.25/ft

*Rates are subject to change, please contact Parks Canada for confirmation.
** Power is available at Burritts Rapids, Merrickville, Upper Brewers and Lower Beveridges lockstations. The price is a fixed $7.00 per 24hr period.
Note: these fees apply to the Rideau Canal, Trent-Severn Waterway and Sault Ste. Marie Canals. In addition, the six day permits and seasonal lockage and mooring permits are valid for all the canals run by Parks Canada in Ontario and Quebec (i.e. with a single season permit you could traverse all those canals).
A **minimum** 12 foot vessel length charge will be made for boats 12 feet and under. Purchase of a mooring permit includes one **free tent site**.
Senior's Discount - Free permits will be issued to Seniors (those born before 1927) to boats they own and operate that are 5.5 m (18'1") and under.
Payment can be made by VISA, Mastercard, personal cheque or cash at any lockstation. Advance purchases can be made by contacting the Rideau Canal Office

Overnight Camping fees

Group Camping	$15/party (up to 10),
	$4.00/add person per party up to 10 persons

Boat Launching and Parking Fees

Boat Launching

Per Launch (includes parking where applicable)......................	$6.00
Season boat launching Poonamalie, Smiths Falls Detached,Edmunds and Beveridges Lock stations	$90.00

Parking

Hogs Back & Long Island Lockstation	$4.00/day $15.00/week $55.00/season
Newboro....................$1.00/day $15.00/week $55.00/season(daily) $100.00/season	
Edmonds and SF Detached	$3.00/day $15.00/week $55.00/season
Black Rapids and Hartwell's	$1.00/hr $4.00/day $15.00/week $55.00/season
Kingston Mills	$1.00/hr $3.00/day $15.00/week $55.00/season

Lockstation Services

	Boater Camping	Washrooms	Public Phones	Water	Boat Launch	Day use Docking	Nautical Charts	Picnic Tables	BBQ Grills	Exhibit/Museum	Self-Guiding Trail
Ottawa locks 1-8		♿	*	✓		✓	✓	✓		✓	
Hartwells 9-10	✓	♿		✓		✓	✓	✓	✓	✓	✓
Hogs back 11-12	✓	♿		✓		✓	✓	✓	✓		✓
Black Rapids 13	✓	♿		✓		✓	✓	✓	✓		
Long Island 14-16	✓	♿	✓	✓		✓	✓	✓	✓		
Burritts Rapids 17	✓	♿		✓		✓	✓	✓	✓		✓
Lower Nicholson 18	✓	✓		✓		✓		✓	✓		
Upper Nicholson 19	✓	♿		✓				✓	✓		
Clowes 20	✓	♿		✓		✓	✓	✓	✓		
Merrickville 21-23	✓	✓	*	✓		✓	✓	✓		✓	
Kilmarnock 24	✓	♿		✓	✓	✓		✓			
Edmunds 25	✓	♿		✓	✓			✓			
Old Slys 26-27	✓	♿		✓				✓	✓		
Smiths Falls 29a	✓	♿	*	✓		✓	✓	✓	✓	✓	✓
Smiths Falls Det. 31	*	♿		✓	✓	✓	✓	✓	✓		
Poonamalie 32	✓	♿		✓	✓			✓			
Upper Beveridges 33	✓	♿		✓		✓		✓			✓
Lower Beveridges 34	✓	♿		✓	✓	✓		✓	✓		
Col. By Island	✓	✓		✓		✓	✓	✓	✓		✓
Narrows 35	✓	✓		✓		✓	✓	✓	✓		
Newboro 36	✓	♿		✓	✓	✓	✓	✓	✓		
Chaffey's 37	✓	♿		✓	✓	✓	✓	✓	✓	✓	
Davis 38	✓	♿		✓				✓	✓		
Jones Falls 39-42	✓	♿	✓	✓		✓	✓	✓	✓	✓	✓
Upper Brewers 43-44	✓	✓		✓				✓	✓		
Lower Brewers 45	✓	♿		✓				✓	✓		
Kingston Mills 46-49	✓	♿	✓	✓		✓	✓	✓	✓	✓	

▲ Boater Camping
ⁿ Washrooms ♿ where indicated
☎ Public Phones
🚰 Water (check w/lockstaff for potability
⛴ Boat Launch
⚙ Day use Docking
🗺 Nautical Charts
🎪 Picnic Tables
🍖 BBQ Grills
🏠 Exhibit/Museum
👫 Self-Guiding Trail

indicates service located nearby

Lockstation Latitude Longitude

Lockstation	Latitude	Longitude
Kingston Mills - bottom	N 44o 17.494'	W 076o 26.572'
Kingston Mills -top	N 44o 17.584'	W 076o 26.497'
Lower Brewers	N 44o 23.373'	W 076o 19.482'
Upper Brewers	N 44o 24.793'	W 076o 18.782'
Jones Falls - lower	N 44o 32.703'	W 076o 14.221'
Jones Falls - upper	N 44o 32.833'	W 076o 14.346'
Davis	N 44o 33.773'	W 076o 17.542'
Chaffey's	N 44o 34.704'	W 076o 19.182'
Newboro	N 44o 38.764'	W 076o 19.252'
Lower Beveridges	N 44o 52.513'	W 076o 08.376'
Upper Beveridges	N 44o 52.623'	W 076o 08.731'
Narrows	N 44o 42.254'	W 076o 17.712'
Poonamalie	N 44o 53.568'	W 076o 03.316'
Smiths Falls Detached	N 44o 53.768'	W 076o 01.616'
Smiths Falls Combined	N 44o 53.803'	W 076o 01.271'
Old Slys	N 44o 53.603'	W 076o 00.251'
Edmonds	N 44o 52.663'	W 075o 59.031'
Kilmarnock	N 44o 53.063'	W 075o 55.806'
Merrickville	N 44o 54.978'	W 075o 50.251'
Clowes	N 44o 56.783'	W 075o 49.361'
Upper Nicholsons	N 44o 57.068'	W 075o 49.031'
Lower Nicholsons	N 44o 57.313'	W 075o 48.976'
Burritts Rapids	N 44o 58.968'	W 075o 47.206'
Long Island Top	N 45o 14.953'	W 075o 41.940'
Long Island Bottom	N 45o 15.113'	W 075o 42.140'
Black Rapids	N 45o 19.303'	W 075o 41.910'
Hogs Back	N 45o 22.213'	W 075o 41.920'
Hartwells	N 45o 23.063'	W 075o 41.995'
Ottawa - top	N 45o 25.403'	W 075o 41.515'

* The data above should not be used for navigation purposes.

The appropriate charts must be used for navigation and the Rideau channel is clearly marked with buoys.

This GPS data can be used for daily trip planning.

Lockstation Phone Numbers

Kingston Mills -	613-542-0622	Old Slys -	613-283-2663
Lower Brewers -	613-542-2629	Edmonds -	613-283-4406
Upper Brewers -	613-387-3564	Kilmarnock -	613-283-3792
Jones Falls -	613-359-5340	Merrickville -	613-269-4787
Davis -	613-359-5620	Clowes -	613-269-4426
Chaffey's -	613-359-5914	Upper Nicholson's -	613-269-4631
Newboro -	613-272-2575	Lower Nicholson's -	613-269-4960
Narrows -	613-272-2700	Burritts Rapids -	613-258-4510
Upper Beveridges -	613-267-2036	Long Island -	613-692-3030
Lower Beveridges -	613-267-2036	Black Rapids -	613-226-5434
Poonamalie -	613-283-3543	Hogs Back -	613-224-5033
Smiths Falls Det. -	613-283-0496	Hartwells -	613-235-2644
Smiths Falls Comb. -	613-283-2103	Ottawa -	613-237-2309

Lockstation Mooring

Blue Line mooring is only available to vessels awaiting lockage. Greyline is available for day-use and overnight mooring. At the lockmaster's discretion, blueline may be used for overnight mooring but vessels are required to leave by first lockage.

Approaching a Lock

The "Blue Line" is a painted blue strip on the concrete walls above and below each lock. By stopping at the Blue Line you indicate to the lock staff that you wish passage through. Three toots of your horn will also alert lock and bridge staff to your intentions. Remain securely tied up until the lock staff instruct you otherwise. At some locks, a green traffic light will be your signal to proceed into the lock chamber.

- Move off the Blue Line in order as indicated by lock staff.
- Houseboats are particularly susceptible to the whims of the wind, so be aware of wind speed and direction, and listen to the advice of lock staff as you enter the lock.
- Your crew (adults, if possible) should be posted at bow and stern and have their lines nearby, neatly coiled and free of knots. Concentrate on coming in straight, using the reverse gear of your motor to slow down.
- As you near the black holding cables attached to the walls of the lock chamber, have your crew members ready to loop, NOT TIE, their lines around the cables. On busy days, it may be necessary to loop your lines to a neighbouring boat.
- Be alert to other boats entering behind you and move forward if necessary. **Do not fend a moving boat off a wall with your hands or feet.** It can lead to serious injury. Use a boat hook. Tend vessel lines carefully.
- Once safely positioned inside the lock chamber, **turn off your engine and do not smoke or use open-flame appliances (no pilot lights).**
- Never leave your boat unattended in the lock. Leave bilge blower on.
- When lock operation is complete and lock gates are opened, wait for staff to direct you to start your engine. Make sure all vessel lines are returned to the boat and exit slowly. REMEMBER to watch out for winds, currents and other boats.
- Be prepared to show your permit to lock staff or be ready to purchase one from them.

Proper Cable Looping

Safety in Historic Canals and Locks

- Ensure boat is equipped with good mooring lines and floating fenders in sufficient size and number are securely fastened.

- Note that the following activities are not permitted while in a canal: excessive noise between 11:00 p.m. and 6:00 a.m.; fishing within 10 m/22 feet of a lock or approach wharf or fishing from a bridge that passes over a navigation channel; diving, jumping, scuba-diving, and swimming in a navigation channel within 100 m of a lock structure; waterskiing or other towing activities within 100 m of a lock structure; mooring a vessel to any navigation aid.

Important **VHF** frequencies are Weatheradio Canada on VHF bands 162.400,162.475 and 162.550MHz. Canadian Coast Guard monitors VHF Marine Channel 16 (156.8 MHz) on a 24 hour basis for safety and emergencies only. They monitor channel 22A (157.1 MHz) for regular calls. Most marinas monitor VHF channel 68 and other pleasure boats use 68 and 71.

GPS (Global Positioning System) units are not required on the Rideau. If you follow the charts it is difficult to get lost but it is a handy device allowing you to locate your position at any given time and make notes of favourite spots. See page 240 for Rideau. If you are travelling here through the St. Lawrence or Lake Ontario GPS is a must.

U.S. Visitor Information

CANPASS for Private Boats: This pass allows visitors from the U.S. on private pleasure boats to clear customs and immigration more quickly. This is particularly appealing if you are frequent visitors. To qualify one must be a citizen or permanent resident of Canada or the United States, pass a strict security check, and pay an annual fee. Once you are a member of the CANPASS program it is very easy to use. The boat's master must report the estimated time of arrival (ETA) by calling 1-888-CANPASS (1-888-226-7277) at any time up to four hours before arriving in Canada. If the 1-888 service is not available, boaters can call the normal business number in Lansdowne, Ontario at (613) 659-4576. Next you declare goods and any duty or tax they owe on goods purchased. This is charged directly to VISA or Mastercard.

To apply for the program visit a customs office or contact 1-800-461-9999. Visit website: cbsa-asfc.gc.ca for more information.

• When private pleasure boats enter Canada, they report to customs by telephone. Private boaters must dock at an approved marine telephone reporting site in Canada (Kingston Mills) and call the telephone reporting centre (TRC) immediately on arrival. 1-888-226-7277. If the 1-888 service is not available, boaters can call the normal business number for the appropriate TRC. Lansdowne, Ontario: (613) 659-4576 The boat's master has to provide the TRC with the following information:
• location of docking site;
• vessel registration number;
• final destination in Canada;
• the full name, date of birth, and citizenship of all persons on board;
• purpose of the trip and length of stay in Canada for non-residents;
• length of absence from Canada for Canadian residents;
• and a customs declaration for each person on board.

All travellers on board must declare any personal goods they are importing, including firearms and weapons, and report all currency and monetary instruments of a value equal to or greater than CAN$10,000

The customs inspector at the TRC will either provide the boater with a clearance number and permission to proceed to the final destination or instruct the boater to remain aboard the vessel until an inspector arrives to complete the examination. Other than the master proceeding to a telephone to report, no traveller can leave the vessel until authorized to do so by customs.

For further information within Canada, call:Canadian Border Services Agency at 1 800 461-9999 (toll free) If you are outside Canada, call (204) 983-3500 or (506) 636-5064 for more information on telephone reporting for vessels. http://www.cbsa-asfc.gc.ca/travel/canpass/menu-e.html

General Info. 1-800-461-9999, Licensing Pleasure Boats 416-973-8027, Boat Registration 416-973-8142.

The *Office of Boating Safety* of the **Canadian Coast Guard** provides information to visiting boaters about requirements for recreational vessels, licensing, exemptions and equipment. Visit their web-site for details call 1-800-267-6687 in Canada or 1-613-991-9002 outside Canada. www.boatingsafety.gc.ca

A foreign boater wishing to use their VHF radio within Canada requires a valid ship's license and an operator license. For information contact **American FCC** at 1-888-CALLFCC www.fcc.gov or the Office of Boating Safety, above for up to date VHF regulations.

When you leave Canada, you may be eligible for a tax refund on the goods you bought in Canada if you take them out of the country within 60 days. For more information, get a copy of the pamphlet called Tax Refund for Visitors to Canada or call 1-800-66VISIT (1-800-668-4748) or (902) 432-5608 (outside Canada). **Canada Revenue Agency**, Write to: Visitor Rebate Program Summerside Tax Centre Canada Customs and Revenue Agency, 275 Pope Road, Suite 104, Summerside, PE C1N 6C6 CANADA or visit web-site http://www.cra-arc.gc.ca/visitors/. Be sure to pick up a copy of the *TAX Refund for Visitors to Canada* Booklet upon entering Canada.

General Government of Canada Information Phone 1-800-762-6232 (800-O-Canada) or visit www.gc.ca

Travelling with **Pets**: if you plan to bring your pet remember to carry a rabies vaccination certificate dated within the last year. Dogs must be licensed and leashed almost everywhere while in Canada and picking up after your pet is law in most places.

Firearms must be declared before entry into Canada. Only weapons for legitimate sporting or recreational use are allowed. In Ontario rifles and shotguns are not permitted outside of hunting season. Other weapons are prohibited and strict penalties apply.

Charts for the Rideau 1512 and 1513 are available through various American distributors a list can be obtained from the **Canadian Hydrographic** web-site:www.charts.gc.ca or by contacting the **Friends of the Rideau** at 1 Jasper Ave., Smiths Falls, Ontario, K7A 4B5 613-283-5810 or visit www.rideaufriends.com

See page 7 of this guide for chart dealers and other information sources.

Small Vessel Licensing and Identification

*A*ll recreational vessels under 15 gross tons and powered by an engine 10 horsepower (7.5 kilowatts) or more must be licensed or registered, regardless of where they operate in Canada. The process is free of charge through Canada Customs and Revenue Agency. Call for office nearest to you. Hold to speak to a Customs Officer.

Licenses are available free of charge from Canada Customs. Licensing Pleasure Boats information number is 1 800 461-9999 E-Mail info@dfo-mpo.gc.ca Website:www.tc.gc.ca (416) 973-8027.

Competency of Operators of Pleasure Craft Regulations requires the operators of pleasure craft fitted with a motor to have proof of competency on board at all times. Proof consists of a)valid proof of having taken a boating safety course; b)a pleasure craft operator card from a Canadian Coast Guard accredited course provider; c)a completed boat rental safety checklist (for power-driven rental boats) Check with the Canadian Coast Guard for organizations providing approved training courses - Office of Boating Safety Infoline at 1-800-267-6687 . http://www.tc.gc.ca/

Boating Rules & Regulations

*R*ules and Regulations apply to every vessel in all navigable waters, from canoes to ships. As a boater it is necessary to follow these rules and regulations in order to protect you, your passengers, other boaters and the wildlife habitat of the region. In most cases you will find the rules are common sense and will not be a problem to follow.

Ontario recently became the first province to introduce on-the-spot ticketing and fines for boaters. Enforcement of on-water rules is now much easier for police and safer for all. Fines are hefty upwards of $200 for such infractions as not enough PFDs or speeding and disobeying refuelling regulations.

Don't Drink & Drive
• The rules for impaired boating are the same as those for impaired driving.

- Most boating accidents that involve fatalities are alcohol related.
- One must not operate a vessel while there is contained on board any open liquor not properly stored in accordance with the Liquor Act.
- You may only drink in a boat that is equipped with a washroom, sleeping accommodations and cooking facilities AND it must be properly docked or at anchor.

The Rideau is patrolled by the **Ontario Provincial Police Marine Unit.** The Marine Unit from the County of Leeds and Grenville is responsible for patrolling the waters in the Rideau Region from Newboro Lake to Seeley's Bay and the Lanark County Marine Unit patrols from Upper Rideau Lake to Burritt's Rapids.

Their duties include 24 hour marine response (overdue boaters, marine collisions), enforcement of Historic Canals Act, Small Vessel Regulations, Collision Regulations, Criminal Code and the Liquor Act. They also attend locks during poor weather. Enforcement of the Fish and Wildlife Conservation Act is the responsibility of Ontario Ministry of Natural Resources but obvious violations will be referred by the OPP to a conservation officer when necessary.

O.P.P. Marine Unit's 24 Hour Emergency Com Centre for Seeley's Bay to Burritt's Rapids call **1-888-310-1122 or use VHF 16.**

Rideau North - (Upper Rideau to Burritt's Rapids) Lanark County Marine Unit during business hours call 613-267-2626.

Rideau South - (Newboro Lake to Seeley's Bay) Leeds & Grenville Count Marine Unit during business hours 613-382-2195.

There are restrictions against pumping sewage into all waters in the province of Ontario. In these areas, a pleasure craft fitted with a toilet must also be fitted with a holding tank and if fitted with a piping system that allows the discharge of sewage directly overboard, then this discharge must be visibly disconnected. Sewage may only be discharged at shore pump-out facilities. Pump-out facilities are available at many marinas. Washroom facilities are available at most lockstations allowing you to cut down on using on-board facilities.

Refuelling

Refuelling requires a number of precautions to be taken:

• Turn off engine; turn off all electrical circuits; douse open flames, including pilot lights; close ports and deck hatches

• Ensure everyone is ashore before fuelling

• Tie boat securely to dock

• No smoking anywhere near refuelling area

• Hold nozzle against filler fitting to prevent sparks

• Do not overfill.

• Boats with inboard motors should have bilge blower turned on for at least 5 minutes prior to starting up after refuelling.

• Check for fumes to make sure bilge is free of gas fumes before starting up.

Mobile Phones can ignite fuel or fumes. Mobile phones that light up when switched on or when they ring release enough energy to provide a spark for ignition. Mobile phones should not be used in filling stations, or when fueling lawn mowers, boat, etc.

| Turn engine off | No open flames | No smoking | Leave bilge blower on |

Right of Way

Collision Avoidance

• Maintain a proper look-out and use every available means to avoid collision.

• Know and understand **'right of way'** rules for power-driven vessels:

Port: if a power driven vessel approaches within this sector maintain course and speed with caution.

Starboard: If any vessel approaches within this sector keep out of its way (may not apply if one or both boats are sailboats)

Stern: If any vessel approaches this sector maintain course and speed with caution.

~Two vessels approaching head on each alter course to starboard and pass port to port. (One horn blast indicates altering to starboard, 5 blasts indicates a problem)

~Any vessel overtaking another must keep clear.

~A power driven vessel keeps clear of a sailing vessel.

• In narrow channels smaller vessels must not get in the way of larger vessels that can only navigate safely within the channel. 5 short blasts of the horn will serve as a reminder to the smaller vessel.

Safe Speed

• It is the operators responsibility to adopt a safe speed, meaning one that allows proper and effective action to be taken to avoid collision.

• The operator must be able to stop their boat within an appropriate distance to the prevailing conditions.

• To determine safe speed consider the following:
visibility, wind, water conditions, currents, and how easy it is to manoeuvre the vessel, traffic density, type and proximity of other ves-

sels, proximity of navigational hazards.

- The operator is responsible for the wake created. One must not create wake that will adversely affect other vessels, shorelines, docks and other users of the waterway including divers and swimmers.

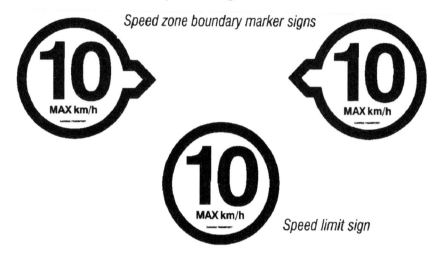

Speed zone boundary marker signs

Speed limit sign

Speed Restrictions

- Shoreline speed restrictions 10km/h within 30metres from shore. Exceptions: waterskiing, where the vessel follows a trajectory perpendicular to the shore; or in rivers of less than 100m in width; or canals, or buoyed channels; or in waters where another speed is prescribed .

- Failure to comply with speed limits results in ticketing or summons.

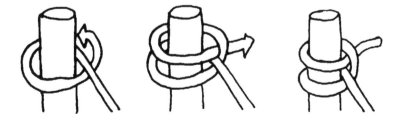

Clove Hitch: This knot, which pulls against itself is used for temporary hitches to docks. It is readily tied and untied.

Navigation Markers

- **Port** (green can, green pillar, green spar) Keep on port (left) side when proceeding upstream.

- **Bifurcation** (red and green bands) You may pass this buoy on either side when proceeding in the upstream direction, but the preferred channel is indicated by the topmost band.

- **Starboard** (red spar, red conical, red pillar)Keep this buoy on starboard (right) side when proceeding upstream

- Isolated Danger buoys are used to mark natural dangers (check with chart)

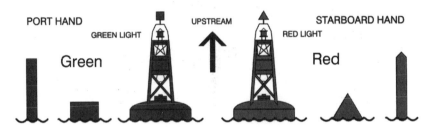

- **"Red Right Returning"** is a basic rule of thumb, which means that while in the navigation channel the red coloured buoys should be on your right(starboard) side when you are returning upstream to home port.

- On the Rideau we have two upstream directions. Newboro is the homeport in both instances. Kingston to Newboro is upstream-when travelling in this direction markers will have red buoys on the right and green on the left. Past Newboro the buoys will be reversed. Newboro to Ottawa is downstream-red on the left and green on the right. This is made clear on the navigational charts.

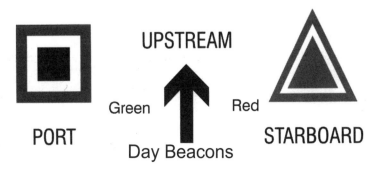

- A boater is legally responsible for operating and equipping a boat safely and for ensuring the safety of those on board.

- A boater is expected to know the rules and regulations that apply to Canadian waterways. Failure to do so results in penalties or fines.

- It is important that PFDs and lifejackets be worn while boating.

- Every boat must carry mandatory safety equipment (PFD for each person etc.)and this list varies depending on the size of your boat. Don't Forget:

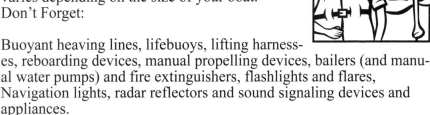

Buoyant heaving lines, lifebuoys, lifting harnesses, reboarding devices, manual propelling devices, bailers (and manual water pumps) and fire extinguishers, flashlights and flares, Navigation lights, radar reflectors and sound signaling devices and appliances.

For a complete list of required equipment contact the Office of Boating Safety.

- Some additional equipment is advised: full set of boat fenders for both sides of boat (at proper height) two boat hooks, two good quality ropes for securing the bow and stern to the lock drop cables - ropes should be supple, 20' long. Good quality mooring line is best. For larger boats a set of small fenders hanging from deckline is recommended to prevent damage in lock when larger fenders are hung to low.

Other suggested items to include:
Tool Kit, Spare Parts, First Aid Kit, Extra Clothing
Drinking Water & High Energy Snacks

For more detailed information contact **Office of Boating Safety** at 1-800-267-6687-in Canada, 1-613-991-1313 outside Canada or visit Web-site: www.tc.gc.ca Office of Boating Safety, Canadian Coast Guard, 200 Kent Street, 13th Floor, Ottawa, Ontario, K1A 0E6

Emergency Assistance

𝔅 oating search and rescue operations in Ontario are jointly co-ordinated by the Ontario Provincial Police, the Department of National Defense (CFB Trenton), the Canadian Coast Guard and other agencies.

Cell Phone Users: Call *OPP (*677) to reach the nearest OPP detachment. With a cellular phone, you may contact Rescue Coordination Centers directly. Or, by dialing *16, you will contact the nearest Canadian Coast Guard Marine Communications Center.

O.P.P 24 hour emergency Com Centre can be reached by calling 1-888-310-1122. In addition, you can reach the Rescue Co-ordination Centre in Trenton by calling 1-800-267-7270.

VHF Radio Users: The Coast Guard monitors VHF Channel 16 (156.8 MHz) VHF Radio Users: Please note that there is **no** continuous monitoring of VHF channel 16 on the Rideau Canal. Channel 16 is used for EMERGENCY and CALLING purposes only. If possible, take your conversation to a working frequency once you have called another vessel on channel 16.

CB Radio Users: Channel 9 is monitored by various agencies for emergency assistance.

In an emergency, the distress call **MAYDAY** is used to indicate the station sending the call is in grave and imminent danger and requires immediate assistance. The message, **PANPAN** is used to indicate the sender requires help on an urgent basis but is not in grave and imminent danger.

WEATHER: Environment Canada weather offices offer a 24 hour a day automated telephone service for the most recent forecast information. You can reach this service in Kingston at (613) 389-3252 and in Ottawa at (613) 998-3439.
Weatheradio Canada provides the most up to date warning and forecast information available and repeats every 5 to 7 minutes. This information is broadcast over three dedicated VHF-FM bands: 162.400, 162.475, and 162.550.
Canadian Coast Guard radio broadcasts marine forecasts in a continuous cycle on VHF bands 161.65 MHz and 161.775 MHz (ch.21B, ch.83B). They also broadcast information on aids to navigation.

$\mathscr{L}$ocks are used to raise and lower boats only a short distance. They operate on a fairly simple principle; water will always find its own level. Locks were the solution to rapids, shallow rocky areas, and other situations which made river navigation problematic. A lock in a canal is essentially a dam, and it keeps the water at the top and bottom from flowing too fast. To get the boat up or down the required elevation it floats the boat in a tub of water. No power is needed. To get the boat up water is let into the "tub" from the upstream side. To get a boat down, water is simply let out of the "tub" on the downstream side. When a boat enters a lock, the gate closes behind it so that the boat is enclosed on all sides. This enclosure is called a chamber. Valves are contained within the walls and gates of the chamber which can be opened or closed, allowing water to enter the chamber from upriver or leave the chamber and flow downriver.

If a boat is travelling upriver, the valves upriver are opened until the water level within the chamber rises and finally equals the elevation of the water upriver. The upriver lock gates are then opened and the boat departs. When a boat travelling downriver enters the lock, the upriver gates close and the downriver valves are opened. This enables the water level of the chamber to recede until it is level with the lower waters. The downriver gates then open and the boat departs. Sometimes, conventional locks are built in a series of two or more and are referred to as flight locks. They can raise or lower boats in stages over a greater height. An example of this can be seen at Ottawa where eight locks operate in flight.

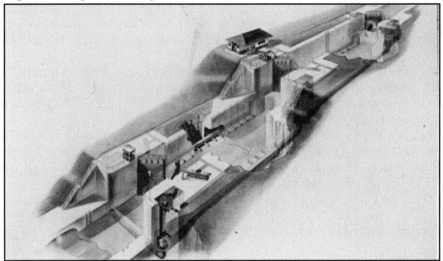

Lockmasters

℗robably one of the most important elements of the Rideau Canal Waterway, apart from the water, is the network of lockmasters. The people who oversee and operate the locks are responsible for keeping everything running smoothly. That is no easy task, especially at popular locks during peak tourist season, foresight, extreme organization, lots of patience and a sense of humour are necessary.

Most of the lockstaff are native to the area they serve and know the waters very well. During the summer, they work long days. They can answer just about any question about the Rideau Canal a boater might pose.

The lovely parklands, campsites, and picnic areas are maintained by the lockmasters and their staff. They are proud of the grounds around their lockstations and their personal interest shows in the well-kept lawns and gardens.

Many people come by car to watch lock operations and this means the lockmasters must work to an audience. Enforcing rules can be difficult under any circumstances, but doing so before an audience can be gruelling, at times.

Lockmasters and their staff are most helpful and work together to ensure our comfort and safety. All locks are connected by phone, so they can alert each other of approaching boats. Your co-operation at the locks contributes to a speedier and safer lock-through for everyone.

Ron Sosnick, Lockmaster at
Upper Beveridges
Photo Credit: Steve Weir,
Rideau Canal, Parks Canada

*I*n order to ensure the future of our waterways and the aquatic environment some enviro-friendly practices are necessary.

• Boaters should be aware that it is an offense to put oil, garbage, or other pollutants into the water, accidentally or willfully, and not report it immediately to the Canadian Coast Guard.

• It is prohibited to dump blackwater (sewage) overboard in all waters of Ontario. Use a pumpout station.

• Keep the following Green Boating Tips on hand and remember to report pollution when you see it.

~keep bilge clean...don't pump oily water overboard
~use bilge sorbents in place of detergents
~use a holding tank
~observe local and federal sewage regulations
~dispose of garbage in appropriate facility... don't litter
~use detergents sparingly, even 'biodegradable' cleansers are hard on the aquatic environment
~don't top off tank while refuelling and clean up spilled fuel
~use only paints approved for marine use
~avoid shoreline erosion, watch wake and propeller wash
~when fishing, practice catch and release

The damage to shoreline habitats is a serious concern. Erosion caused by passing boats causes damage to many creatures. Aquatic ecosystems can be devastated. It is important that every boater be concerned about this. Reducing wake will greatly benefit the shoreline, keep our lakes healthy and make boating safer.

Wash refers to the waves made by a boat passing through the water. Wake is the track left by a boat in the water.

These waves cause damage to people as well as the environment. On top of the devastating impact on shorelines-erosion and the disruption of plants and animals, the swamping of loon nests, waves cause damage to docks, interfere with safe navigation, upset small boats and canoes and cause danger to swimmers. A large wave can cause an undertow, especially close to shore where the water is shallow. This is dangerous to swimmers, especially children. **No one should ever boat near swimmers.**

You can help prevent wake damage by remembering the following:

- Know at what speed your boat produces the least wake

- Go 'dead slow' when close to shore, in busy areas and along narrow channels

- Take extra caution when approaching other traffic

- Take notice of 'Watch Your Wake' signs.

Enforcing "NO WAKE"

In 'No Wake' legislation in the small vessel regulations, the two most important points to consider are 1. protect human life 2. protect property.

The law in Ontario says power boaters must slow down to 10km/hr within 30m of a shore line, faster than that and you may be fined up to $500.00. Personal Watercrafts pose the same threat to shorelines already described.

Note: if your boat lacks a speedometer keep in mind that travelling 10 km/hr or less generates little or no wake

For more information about WASH and preventative measures contact the Friends of the Rideau and obtain a STOP WASH Booklet 1 Jasper Ave., Smiths Falls, On, K7A 4B5 call 1-613-283-5810 or visit their website at www.rideaufriends.com

Depth in navigation channel	1.5 m (5')
Operational size of locks	27.4 (90')L x 8.5m (28')W
Length of Canal	202km (126 miles)
Year Canal opened	1832
Highest lift (of a lock)	7.9m (26') Smiths Falls Combined
Peak navigation season	July & August
Speed limit zones	yes, 6-10 km/hr
Number of locks 47	Number of lock stations 24

Rideau Distance Chart
approximate distance (in miles) by boat
(miles x 2.2 = kms)

5	Kingston
23	18	Kingston Mills
28	23	5	Jones Falls
34	29	11	6	Chaffey's Lock
39	34	16	11	5	Newboro
44	39	21	16	10	5	Narrows
58	53	35	30	24	19	14	Rideau Ferry
59	54	36	31	25	20	15	1	Tay River
64	59	41	36	30	25	20	6	5	Poonamalie
67	62	44	39	33	28	23	9	8	3	Smiths Falls
80	75	57	52	46	41	36	22	21	16	13	Merrickville
86	81	63	58	52	47	42	28	27	22	19	6	Burritt's Rapids
93	88	70	65	59	54	49	35	34	29	26	13	7	Kemptville Creek
100	95	77	72	66	61	56	42	41	36	33	20	14	7	Kars
107	102	84	79	73	68	63	49	48	43	40	27	21	14	7	Manotick
120	115	97	92	86	81	76	62	61	56	53	40	34	27	20	13	Dow's Lake
123	118	100	95	89	84	79	65	64	59	56	43	37	30	23	16	3	Ottawa

FRIENDS OF THE
RIDEAU

People dedicated to preserving and enhancing all those elements that make the Rideau a unique North American Waterway

The Friends of the Rideau is a volunteer, non-profit organization, which works in close co-operation with Parks Canada.

We work to enhance and conserve the heritage and charm of the Rideau Waterway.

We work to increase public awareness and enjoyment of the Rideau Waterway.

We work to develop strong public support for the long-term well being of the Rideau Waterway.

Our membership enjoys:

✓ The knowledge that they are helping to preserve and enhance the scenic Rideau.

✓ Newsletters keeping them up to date about the Rideau Waterway.

✓ Discounts on products sold by Friends of the Rideau.

- -

Yes - I wish to support the activities of Friends of the Rideau

❑ Here is my application for membership

Name: _____

Address:_____

_____

City: _____ Prov: _____ Pcode: _____

Phone (   ) _____

Email: _____

__ Family Membership $20   __ Business Membership $50

Please make cheque payable to: *Friends of the Rideau* and mail to:
Friends of the Rideau, 1 Jasper Avenue, Smiths Falls, Ontario K7A 4B5

visit us in the summer at The Depot in Merrickville (beside the Blockhouse)
or at any time of the year at: www.rideaufriends.com

Visitor Information Services

*I*t is important to preplan your visit to the Rideau Waterway. The following resources are available to help you prepare:

www.rideau-info.com
Rideau Canal Waterway Information
A very comprehensive Rideau information source.

REALONTARIO.ca
is a web based reservation and information system for eastern ontario.
Historic Aaron Merrick Block Suite 200, 104 St. Lawrence Street PO Box 730
Merrickville, ON K0G 1N0
Tel: (613) 269-2777 Fax: (613) 269-2942
Email: info@realontario.ca
www.REALONTARIO.ca

Ontario East Tourist Association,
1-800-567-3278 or 613-658-2363
Email: info@ontarioeast.com
Website: www.ontarioeast.com

Rideau Canal HQ Office
34a Beckwith St. S.
Smiths Falls, Ontario K7A 2A8
1-800-230-0016 or 613-283-5170
www.parkscanada.gc.ca/lhn-nhs/on/rideau/

Friends of the Rideau
1 Jasper Ave.
Smiths Falls, Ontario K7A 4B5
613-283-5810
email: info@rideaufriends.com
www.rideaufriends.com

Ontario Marine Operators Assoc.
2 Poyntz St. Suite 49
Penetanguishene, ON L9M 1M2
705-549-1669 Fax: 705-549-1670
email: omoa@marinasontario.com
website: www.marinasontario.com

Canadian Customs Information Unit
P.O. Box 10 Stn 'A'
Toronto, Ontario M5W 1A3
1-800-461-9999 - General Information
Boat Licensing 416-973-8027
Boat Registration 416-973-8142

Transport Canada
Office of Boating Safety
(AMSRO)
330 Sparks Street, 11th Floor
Ottawa, ON
K1A 0N5
Safe Boating Infoline 1-800-267-6687
(in Canada only)
1-613-991-9002 (outside Canada) -
Safe Boating Infoline
www.tc.gc.ca/BoatingSafety/menu.htm

Canadian Hydrographic Service
Dept. Fisheries & Oceans
1675 Russell Road, P.O. Box 8080
Ottawa, Ontario K1G 3H6
613-998-4931
email chs_sales@dfo-mpo.gc.ca
website: www.charts.gc.ca

KEDCO
Kingston Visitor Welcome Centre
209 Ontario St.
Kingston, Ontario K7L 2Z1
613-548-4415 or 1-888-855-4555
email: reception@kingstoncanada.com
website: kingstoncanada.com

Ottawa Tourism & Convention Authority
130 Albert St. Suite 1800
Ottawa, Ontario K1P 5G4
1-800-465-1867 oper. 55
email: info@tourottawa.org
website: www.tourottawa.org

Lyndhurst/Seeley's Bay Chamber of Commerce
Box 89 Lyndhurst, Ontario KOE 1N0
613-387-3847 email:
shaw@kingston.net

Twp of Rear of Leeds & Lansdowne
Seeley's Bay Public Dock, Village info.
P.O. Box 160, Lyndhurst, On K0E 1N0
613-928-2423

Elgin Chamber of Commerce
Box 190, Elgin, Ontario K0G 1E0
613-359-5108
website: www.rideaulakes.net/Elgincc/

Westport & Rideau Lakes Chamber of Commerce
Box 157A, Westport, Ontario K0G 1X0
613-273-2929
email: wrlcc@rideau.net
website:
www.westportrideaulakes.on.ca

Perth Chamber of Commerce
34 Herriot , Perth, Ontario K7H 1T2
613-267-3200 email:
pcoc@superaje.com

Lanark County Tourism Association
Box 37, Sunset Blvd.
Perth, Ontario K7H 3E2
613-267-4200 ext. 142
1-888-452-6275
email: tourism@county.lanark.on.ca
www.lanarkcountytourism.ca/

Smiths Falls Chamber of Commerce
Box 695, Smiths Falls, Ontario
K7A 4T6   1-800-257-1334
or 613-283-1334

Merrickville Chamber of Commerce
Box 571, Merrickville, Ontario
K0G 1N0 613-269-2229

North Grenville Chamber of Commerce
Box 1047 Kemptville, On K0G 1J0
613-258-4838 ext 2039
email: chamberk@cyberus.ca

The Long Reach Association
Box 41 Kars, ON K0A 2E0 Tel: (613)
489-2747 email: longisland@cyberus.ca
website: www.rideau-info.com/longreach/

Rideau Valley Conservation Auth.
1-800-267-3504 or 613-692-3571

Canadian Recreational Canoeing Association
PO Box 398, 446 Main St West
Merrickville ON K0G 1N0   Telephone:
613-269-2910
Toll Free: 1-888-252-6292
www.paddlingcanada.com

Ontario Parks - Rideau River and
Murphy's Point
1-888-ONT-PARK reservations
website: www.ontarioparks.com

Index